# CUPCAKES

## Galore

# CUPCAKES
## Galore

Gail Wagman

spruce

An Hachette UK Company
www.hachette.co.uk

First published in Great Britain in 2006 by Spruce,
a division of Octopus Publishing Group Ltd
Endeavour House
189 Shaftesbury Avenue
London
WC2H 8JY
www.octopusbooks.co.uk
www.octopusbooks.usa.com

This edition published in 2012

Copyright © Octopus Publishing Group Ltd 2006
Text copyright © Gail Wagman 2006

Distributed in the US by
Hachette Book Group USA
237 Park Avenue
New York NY 10017 USA

Distributed in Canada by
Canadian Manda Group
165 Dufferin Street
Toronto, Ontario, Canada M6K 3H6

ISBN 978-1-84601-406-2

A CIP catalogue record for this book is available
from the British Library

Printed and bound in China

10 9 8 7 6 5 4 3 2 1

Photography: Olivier Maynard
Design: Clare Barber

# CONTENTS

Introduction  6

Grandma's Favorites  16

Kids' Cupcakes  40

After Dinner Cupcakes  60

Gourmet Cupcakes  82

Holiday Cupcakes  118

Cupcakes Plus  146

Index  186

# INTRODUCTION

When the idea of writing a book on cupcakes was first broached to me, I immediately had visions of those cupcakes of my youth—the ones my mother used to make for the birthday parties of my childhood.

## ★ ORIGINS ★

You remember—they were usually made with either chocolate or yellow batter, lavished with gobs of pastel frosting and decorated with chocolate sprinkles, coconut, candied fruits, or nuts. They were always served on a big platter with a candle in each one in honor of the birthday girl or boy or brought to school

on that special day to be shared with friends during recess. Cupcakes have of course come a long way since then, thanks to the amazing amount of cupcake paraphernalia available on the market, from decorations to cupcake tins, as well as the many recipes expressly designed for them or that can be adapted to them.
But we will come back to that later. For the time being, let's set the record straight. Just what is a cupcake? And what isn't? Webster's Dictionary defines a cupcake as follows:

**noun:**

*a small cake baked in a cuplike mold*
This minimal definition just about sums it up—no more, no less—leaving a great deal of room for interpretation, creativity, and perhaps a little confusion.

## ★ A CUPCAKE WITH ANY OTHER NAME ... ★

A cupcake is undeniably a "little cake," but all "little cakes" aren't necessarily cupcakes. Unless they are made in a cup-sized mold. And fit the criteria of a "cake," let's say, as opposed to a muffin, which can be made in a cup-sized mold but is basically a quick bread and not a cake. And then again, some cupcake recipes are "quick" but the result is not to be mistaken for a muffin. And does a cupcake require icing to conform to the appellation? Iconographically speaking, I would say yes since the festive character of the beast certainly lends itself to a little "dressing up for the occasion," but it would really be too bad to add anything other than powdered sugar or a little glaze to some of the cupcakes in this book. A number of sources refer to the origin of the humble cupcake as a "cup cake," in other words, a 1 (cup butter)–2 (cups sugar)–3 (cups flour)–4 (eggs) cake, which can certainly be made into cupcakes (provided that you add a little flavoring, a substantial dose of imagination, some yummy frosting, and a decoration or two) but as anyone who has ever made a cake will know, this refers to what is commonly known as a pound cake and no one is mistaking that for a cupcake.

So, if you stick to my definition, you can't go wrong. Just remember the three cardinal rules:

1. cupcakes should be pretty

2. cupcakes should taste good

3. cupcakes should be fun

## ★ THE PARTY BEAST ★

Defining a cupcake is sort of like defining a pair of
shorts (short pants). Or a can of soda (compared to a
bottle). Or a bikini (as opposed to a one-piece bathing
suit). It is just a smaller version of the original that has
taken on a meaning of its own (thus the confusion).
When referring to cupcakes, most of the respectable
cookbooks that I have consulted agree that nearly all
cake batters lend themselves to being baked in
individual portions. My experience has certainly proved
that to be true. It is a rare cake batter that cannot be
metamorphosed into a cupcake with the addition of
some sort of topping or decoration. So I have decided
to stick with my original idea of the cupcake as a
"party beast"—no "savory" cupcakes here—I'll leave
that for the muffin department. My two basic criteria
were (1) the cupcakes all had to be made with some
sort of cake batter (to be defined); and (2) they could
be made in a cupcake tin—either with or without a
paper, mini, regular, or jumbo. I have added an extra
section entitled "Cupcakes Plus" for those "cupcakes"

that may or may not specifically fit those criteria but that can be made in a cupcake tin and/or served in a cupcake paper and that could pass for a cupcake with a little imagination.

I hope you enjoy these recipes. I had great fun writing them and am very excited about sharing them with you. Special thanks to my "testers"—Mark, my son, and his friends at school who received a batch every Monday morning to start off the week, Brigitte and Christian who stopped by on Saturday mornings after the market to try my latest creations and whose detailed tasting notes were invaluable, and to all my other friends who have been on a "cupcake diet" since I started this project. I am forever grateful to Alain, my partner in all culinary endeavors, for having not only tested all of my recipes but for having so patiently listened to the "Cupcake Monologue" during the gestation of this book. And then there is of course my daughter Emily who could leave no cupcake paper unturned and who constantly supplied me with ideas and cupcake paraphernalia while I was writing the book.

# SOME RULES
## of Thumb

Here are a few helpful hints for the aspiring cupcake baker. So put on that apron and get to work!

## ★ RECIPES ★

Almost all of the cupcake recipes in this book (with the exception of some of the ones in the "Cupcakes Plus" section) are really cake recipes tailored to a cupcake. As I already mentioned in the introduction, just about any cake recipe can be used to make a cupcake. Only the cooking time will change which is true within the range of cupcake sizes as well—mini cupcakes will take less time than regular cupcakes that will take less time than jumbo cupcakes that will take less time than a cake. Logical, isn't it? Take your favorite cake recipe, bake it in a cupcake tin, add a little frosting, a glaze, some powdered sugar, and a decoration, and you will have your own original cupcake recipe. Let your imagination be your guide.

## ★ INGREDIENTS ★

As a rule of thumb, all ingredients should be at room temperature unless otherwise indicated (frozen berries, hot milk, etc.). I used all-purpose flour for all of the recipes in this book. If you want to use cake flour, add 2 tablespoons per cup of all-purpose flour. I never use self-rising flour since it already has salt and a leavening agent in it and I prefer to add my own. As for leavening agents, I generally use 1 teaspoon baking powder per cup of flour and fraction thereof. I only use baking soda when there is an acid factor such a buttermilk, sour cream, yogurt, or citrus juice. Otherwise, it apparently serves no purpose. Whenever possible, I mix all of the dry ingredients together before mixing them into the batter. Which brings us to the question—to sift or not to sift? From all that I have read and from my own experience, I don't think sifting adds anything to a recipe except when you are adding small quantities of flour to beaten egg whites with a whisk, allowing you to add the flour slowly and not to deflate the whites. In my old recipe books from the 50s, ingredients are sometimes sifted three times before being measured. I'm not sure what the logic was but I wouldn't waste my time. I only use unsalted butter. I live in France and almost all of the butter available is unsalted. If you are using salted butter, leave the salt out of the recipe. Both salt and cream of tartar are used to stabilize beaten egg whites. Use about $\frac{1}{8}$ teaspoon cream of tartar or a pinch of salt for every 2 egg whites.

## ★ BAKING TIPS ★

Most of the recipes call for the cupcake papers or molds to be filled $\frac{2}{3}$ full. There are exceptions of course. If you are adding a topping, you will probably want to leave more room (Strawberry-Filled Oatmeal Cupcake, for instance). Unless otherwise stated, I generally suggested preheating the oven to 350°F. Some recipes require a hotter or a cooler oven and, occasionally, the temperature has to be turned down while the cupcakes are baking. In that case, just follow the recipe. I tend to bake just about everything in a moderate, preheated oven. Remember that temperatures vary from one oven to the next, so know your oven and use your common sense. There are just so many variables—weather, altitude, position in the oven, whether it is a first or second batch, etc. I generally insert a tester in my cupcakes to see if they are done. When it comes out clean, remove the cupcakes from the oven. Some cupcakes stay moist in the center (Chocolate Mousse, cupcakes cooked with fruit like the Blueberry and Raspberry Cream Cupcake for the Fourth of July), defying the "tester" test. In any case, when they start to burn, regardless of the recipe, you will know that you have left them in the oven too long!

It is generally advisable to let the cupcakes cool before removing them from the tins. Place them on a rack when you take them out of the oven. Some can be unmolded after about 10 minutes whereas the denser ones should be completely cooled first.

Just remember, any rule that applies to cake baking techniques or ingredients generally applies to cupcakes.

# EQUIPMENT

Cupcake paraphernalia can be found in just about any supermarket and in all good kitchen supply stores.

## ★ CUPCAKE TINS ★

Cupcake tins (also known as muffin tins) come in a variety of sizes but the three major sizes are "mini" (1¼ to 2 inches in diameter, holding ⅛ cup or 2 tablespoons batter), "regular" (2½ inches in diameter, holding ¼ to ⅓ cup batter), and "jumbo" (3½ inches in diameter, holding about ⅝ cup batter). The number of cups in the tin is variable. I have mini-cupcake tins with 20 cups and others with 30. There are usually 12 cups in a regular-size cupcake tin whereas the silicon ones are often smaller. My jumbo tins make six jumbo cupcakes each. Tins come in metal, in which case you have to grease and flour them if you are not using cupcake papers. Although I see no reason not to use cupcake papers and avoid the mess. The new silicon molds are very handy and can be used at high temperatures in an oven without any additional

preparation. They are nonstick and the cupcakes will just pop out as soon as they are cool. They come in rigid and nonrigid varieties and are extremely easy to clean. Just remember to use a baking sheet with the nonrigid ones. I prefer metal tins when using cupcake papers and nonstick silicon molds when I am not.

## ★ CUPCAKE PAPERS ★

Cupcake papers come in a variety of colors and designs. I have found ones for just about every occasion—Christmas, Valentine's Day, the Fourth of July, St. Patrick's Day, etc. and for every season—fall leaves and spring flowers, just to name a few. There are papers with Barbie dolls, baseball bats, footballs, and some rather unidentifiable objects. Supermarkets seem to carry the pastel ones of my youth whereas many of the specialty stores carry plain white ones which are good

for any occasion. They also come in a full rainbow of colors and in gold and silver. The variety is slightly more limited for the mini and jumbo versions. And plain papers will do just fine. Remember, it is what is inside and on top that counts.

As for any other equipment you will need to make a cupcake, it is basically the same as what you would need to make a cake—spatula, whisk, wooden spoon, measuring cups and spoons, electric or hand beater, electric mixer, and a wide range of bowl sizes. You will also need some equipment to make frosting and decorations, but I will cover that in the section devoted to those topics.

# DRESSING UP FOR
## the Occasion

Icings, Frosting, Toppings, and Glazes
and, last but not least, Decorations.

### ★ THE CROWNING TOUCH ★

Is a cupcake a cupcake with nothing on top? Since
I'm not quite sure but tend to believe that a cupcake
is the sum of its individual parts, I have given at least
one alternative for every cupcake in this book—
whether it be an icing or frosting as in the majority
of the recipes, a topping as in the case of the Apple
Crumble or Bourdaloue, a glaze for the Kir or Honey
Hazelnut Cupcake, or just a dusting of powdered sugar
for the Poppyseed Cupcake—plus some sort of
decoration. I have used the terms "frosting" and "icing"
interchangeably. Webster's Dictionary gives "icing" as a
synonym for "frosting" and vice versa. I just love the
definition of "icing" in my Webster's Dictionary and you
will see why: "a sweet, flavored and usually creamy
mixture used to coat baked goods (as cupcakes) [sic]—
called also frosting." Can you believe that? So I guess
that cupcakes are just predestined to have some sort of
icing/frosting/topping/glaze. After all, they could have
said "cakes." But no. They explicitly mention cupcakes.
In Alan Davidson's Oxford Companion to Food, he goes
into great detail about "icings" but doesn't mention
"frosting." The Joy of Cooking has a whole section on
"Icings" whereas the Fanny Farmer Cookbook has it all
under "Frostings."

Cake/cupcake icing/frosting is an art in itself. As is
cake/cupcake decorating. Many books exist on the
subject and all good cookbooks will have a section

devoted to the topic as well. I have tried to present a full panoply of alternatives, from the simple to the more complicated—easy-to-make-icings with just powdered sugar and a little liquid, to cooked icings that require a bit more skill and time. Ready-made icings can be found in supermarkets and specialty stores if you are in a hurry although some of the recipes in this book can be made in the time it will take you to open the can or read the directions on the ready-made stuff. Fondant is a challenge to even the most skilled baker and I always use one of the brands available on the market. with the addition of a little sugar syrup, flavoring, and coloring, if need may be. Feel free to mix and match as well. And create your own personalized versions by changing the flavors. For example, replace the mint in the Mint Butter Cream Frosting with lavender or lemon extract, or a few drops of orange flower water or rose water, and invent your own recipes. A little imagination will go a long way.

And speaking of imagination—a word on cupcake decorations! I guess you could just say "awesome." On a recent trip to the States, I was astounded and impressed by the quantity of decorations available on the market. I mean, there is just no excuse for an ugly cupcake at this point in civilization. Glitter sugars, colored sugars, every shape and size of sprinkles for every occasion, instant decorator tubes in every color of the rainbow, colored sprays, edible decorations in the form of flowers, clowns, footballs—you name it—plus all the rest including candied, dried, and jellied fruits, nuts, gummy candies, miniature candies, and cookies— and those are just some of the obvious ones. So, in the spirit of that party beast known as the cupcake—free your inner "cupcake decorator"—and have a ball.

# GRANDMA'S
## FAVORITES

# ZUCCHINI PINE NUT
## Cupcakes

This is one way of using up some of that extra zucchini and getting your kids to eat it too. They'll never know but they will surely ask for seconds. And it will be a great hit with adults as well.

**MAKES: ABOUT 12–14 CUPCAKES**

1½ cups shredded zucchini
1⅓ cups all-purpose flour
2 teaspoons baking powder
1 teaspoon salt
1 cup ground almonds
1 egg
⅔ cup sugar
⅔ cup heavy cream
⅓ cup vegetable oil
½ cup pine nuts

CREAM CHEESE FROSTING
1 cup powdered sugar
4 ounces cream cheese, softened
1 egg white, slightly beaten
Pinch of salt
1 teaspoon vanilla extract
½ cup pine nuts for decoration

1. Preheat oven to 350°F.

2. In a large bowl, mix together zucchini, flour, baking powder, salt, and ground almonds.

3. In another bowl, mix the egg, sugar, cream, oil, and pine nuts. Pour this batter into the first one and blend well with a whisk or a wooden spoon.

4. Fill cupcake papers about ¾ full and cook for 20–25 minutes or until a tester inserted into the center comes out clean. Remove from the oven and cool.

5. Beat all the frosting ingredients together until light and of good spreading consistency. Frost the cooled cupcakes and sprinkle a few pine nuts over each cupcake before serving. Alternatively, dust the cooled cupcakes with powdered sugar.

**CUPCAKE TIP**
*If you don't have pine nuts, use either walnuts or hazelnuts.*

# CHOCOLATE COCONUT
## Cupcakes

Instant chocolate pudding was a staple of my childhood. My mother would make it as a special treat, to be eaten slowly, treasuring every mouthful. These cupcakes are a tribute to that time long ago and the coconut is my little personal touch.

**MAKES: ABOUT 12–14 CUPCAKES**

1²⁄₃ cups all-purpose flour
2 teaspoons baking powder
1 teaspoon salt, plus pinch for egg whites
3 eggs, separated
¹⁄₂ cup brown sugar
¹⁄₂ cup vegetable oil, plus 2 tablespoons
1 cup shredded coconut, plus 2 tablespoons for dusting
2 tablespoons unsweetened cocoa powder
4 ounces dark chocolate, grated
4 tablespoons milk
Chocolate pudding (instant, ready-made or homemade)
Whipped cream, for decoration
Powdered chocolate or cocoa powder, for dusting

1. Preheat oven to 350°F.

2. Mix flour, baking powder, and salt and set aside.

3. With a whisk or a wooden spoon, mix egg yolks and sugar together. Add oil and then flour mixture, beating until batter is smooth. Mix in coconut, cocoa powder, grated chocolate, and milk and blend well.

4. Using an electric beater, beat egg whites with a pinch of salt until stiff but not dry. Gently fold into chocolate batter.

5. Spoon batter into cupcake papers, filling about ²⁄₃ full. Smooth batter with the back of a spoon. Sprinkle a little coconut over each cupcake. Cook for 10 minutes and then lower temperature to 300°F and cook for another 20 minutes or until a tester inserted into the center comes out clean. Remove from oven and cool.

6. When cupcakes are completely cool, cut a circle or cone out of the top with an apple corer and heap chocolate pudding in it. Add a little dollop of whipped cream for decoration. Dust with powdered chocolate or cocoa powder.

# BLACK & WHITE
## Cupcakes

Native New Yorkers will be familiar with these cupcakes although they are traditionally found in cookie form at delicatessens throughout the U.S.

**MAKES: ABOUT 16 CUPCAKES**

CHOCOLATE & VANILLA
MARBLE CUPCAKE
1½ cups all-purpose flour
2 teaspoons baking powder
1 teaspoon salt, plus pinch for the
 egg whites
6 tablespoons/¾ stick unsalted
 butter, room temperature
1 cup sugar
2 eggs, separated
⅓ cup whole milk
1 teaspoon vanilla extract
1 tablespoon unsweetened cocoa
 powder
BLACK & WHITE ICING
2 cups powdered sugar
¼ cup boiling water (more or less,
 depending on spreading
 consistency)
1 ounce dark chocolate
Chocolate buttons for decoration

1. Preheat oven to 350°F. Mix dry ingredients together in a bowl. Set aside.

2. In the large bowl of an electric mixer, cream butter and sugar until light and fluffy. Add egg yolks and beat to blend. Alternately add dry ingredients and milk, beating well after each addition.

3. Divide batter into two separate bowls. Mix the vanilla into one of the batters and cocoa powder into the other.

4. Beat egg whites with a pinch of salt until they form stiff peaks. Divide in half and gently fold half into each of the two batters.

5. Spoon batter into cupcake papers, filling cups about ⅔ full, 1 heaping teaspoon at a time, alternating batters. They will appear not to be mixed but will "marble" when cooked. Bake for 25 minutes or until a tester inserted into the center comes out clean. Remove from oven and cool.

6. To make the icing: place powdered sugar in a medium-size bowl. Gradually mix in boiling water, 1 tablespoon at a time. Mixture should be very thick but easy to spread. Divide mixture into two parts.

7. Put half the icing in a double boiler with the chocolate over simmering (not boiling) water. Stir and remove from heat as soon as the chocolate is melted. While icing is warm to the touch, spread on cupcakes—half white, half chocolate. Place a chocolate button in the center of each cupcake.

# BLUE BLUEBERRY 'N' CREAM Cupcakes

The "trick," for these cupcakes is to defrost the blueberries until they became mushy so that they impart their blue color to the batter.

**MAKES: ABOUT 18 REGULAR CUPCAKES OR 8 JUMBO CUPCAKES**

2½ cups all-purpose flour
3 teaspoons baking powder
1 teaspoon salt
½ cup/1 stick unsalted butter, room temperature
1 cup sugar
2 eggs
1 cup milk or light cream
¾ cup blueberries (if you are using frozen blueberries, defrost beforehand), plus ½ cup frozen or fresh blueberries
1 tablespoon water

BLUE BLUEBERRY WHIPPED CREAM
1 cup whipping cream
¼ cup sugar
¼ cup reserved crushed blueberries (see method)
Dried blueberries (optional) for decoration

1. Preheat oven to 350°F. Mix flour, baking powder, and salt together and set aside.

2. In the large bowl of an electric mixer, cream butter and sugar until light and fluffy. Add eggs, one at a time, beating well after each addition. Alternately add dry ingredients and milk or cream.

3. Using a fork, crush ¾ cup blueberries with 1 tablespoon water until they are soft. Save ¼ cup for the frosting. Add ½ cup to the batter and blend thoroughly. Batter will be blue. Gently fold in remaining ½ cup blueberries.

4. Spoon batter into cupcake papers, filling cups about ⅔ full. Cook for 20–25 minutes or until a tester inserted into the center comes out clean. Remove from oven and cool.

5. To make the whipped cream: with an electric beater, beat cream until it starts to form soft peaks. Gradually add sugar, beating constantly. Add crushed blueberries and beat until stiff.

6. Frost cupcakes and sprinkle with dried blueberries, if desired. These cupcakes should be frosted just before serving. Alternatively, because of their beautiful color, you can leave them as is and dust them with powdered sugar.

# BROWNIE Cupcakes

This recipe is dedicated to Julien, who is my biggest brownie fan, no matter what form they come in!

**MAKES: ABOUT 12 CUPCAKES**

1 cup all-purpose flour
1 teaspoon baking powder
1 teaspoon salt
6 ounces dark chocolate, broken into pieces
6 tablespoons/¾ stick unsalted butter, room temperature, cut into pieces
¾ cup sugar
2 eggs
1 teaspoon vanilla extract
1 cup chopped walnuts

 WALNUT FUDGE FROSTING
3 ounces dark chocolate, cut into pieces
1 cup sugar
⅓ cup milk
3 tablespoons unsalted butter
1 tablespoon corn syrup
Pinch of salt
1 teaspoon vanilla extract

FOR DECORATION
½ cup chopped walnuts (optional) or 12 walnut halves
Chocolate buttons

1. Preheat oven to 350°F.

2. Mix flour, baking powder, and salt together and set aside.

3. Place chocolate, butter, and sugar in a large bowl over simmering water. Heat until just melted, stirring from time to time (do not cook). This will only take a few minutes. Remove from heat. Add eggs, one at a time, blending well after each addition. Add vanilla. Gradually add dry ingredients. When batter is smooth and dry ingredients have been absorbed, fold in chopped walnuts.

4. Divide batter between 12 cupcake papers, smoothing with the back of a spoon. Cook for about 20–25 minutes. Cupcakes should form a crust on top and be a little moist inside. Remove from oven and cool completely before removing from tin.

5. To make the frosting: place all of the ingredients except the vanilla and walnuts in a heavy pan. Bring to a full boil and cook for 1 minute, stirring constantly. Remove from heat and cool (you can set bowl in cold water to speed up the process).

6. Add vanilla and beat until thick, about 10 minutes, until frosting is fluffy and the color has slightly lightened. If you are using chopped walnuts in the frosting, fold them in now. Frost cooled cupcakes. Top each cupcake with a walnut halves and a chocolate button.

# CHOCOLATE PEANUT BUTTER Cupcakes

Peanut butter and chocolate are one of those fabulous duos, immortalized in many children's candies and traditional desserts.

**MAKES: ABOUT 18 CUPCAKES**

2 cups all-purpose flour
2 teaspoons baking powder
1 teaspoon salt
2 ounces good quality dark chocolate
$^{1}/_{4}$ cup/$^{1}/_{2}$ stick unsalted butter, room temperature
4 tablespoons smooth peanut butter
1 cup sugar
2 eggs
$^{3}/_{4}$ cup milk
1 cup peanut chocolate chips (optional)

FROSTING

3 ounces milk chocolate
$^{1}/_{4}$ cup/$^{1}/_{2}$ stick unsalted butter, cut into small pieces
1$^{2}/_{3}$ cups powdered sugar
Pinch of salt
$^{1}/_{4}$ cup heavy cream
1 teaspoon vanilla extract
3 tablespoons smooth peanut butter
Peanut-chocolate candies (peanut M&M's, Reese's Pieces etc.)

1. Preheat oven to 350°F.

2. Mix flour, baking powder, and salt together and set aside.

3. Melt chocolate in a double boiler or microwave. Set aside and cool.

4. In the large bowl of an electric mixer, cream butter, peanut butter, and sugar until light and fluffy. Add eggs, one at a time, mixing well after each addition. Add cooled chocolate and blend well. Alternately beat in dry ingredients and milk.

5. Spoon batter into cupcake papers, filling cups about $^{2}/_{3}$ full. Sprinkle a few peanut chocolate chips over each cupcake, gently pressing them into the batter with a fork. Bake for 25 minutes or until a tester comes out clean. Remove from oven and cool.

6. To make the frosting: heat chocolate and butter in a double boiler or a microwave until just melted.

7. Remove from heat and cool. Using a whisk or a wooden spoon, beat sugar, salt, cream, and vanilla until smooth. Add cooled chocolate mixture and peanut butter and beat until blended. Put the frosting in the refrigerator until it thickens (about 20–30 minutes).

8. Remove from refrigerator, beat until frosting is of spreading consistency and frost cooled cupcakes. Decorate with peanut-chocolate candies.

# LEMON MERINGUE PIE Cupcakes

These lemon meringue cupcakes will add an elegant touch to the end of any meal. Lemon desserts are always a favorite because of their tart flavor. Add this one to your repertory.

**MAKES: ABOUT 12 CUPCAKES**

1½ cups all-purpose flour
2 teaspoons baking powder
1 teaspoon salt
2 tablespoons grated lemon rind
½ cup/1 stick unsalted butter
1 cup sugar
2 eggs
2 tablespoons lemon juice

LEMON CREAM
¾ cup sugar
3 tablespoons all-purpose flour
Pinch of salt
¼ cup lemon juice
Grated rind of 1 lemon
½ cup water
3 egg yolks, beaten (save whites for
    meringue)
2 tablespoons/¼ stick unsalted butter

MERINGUE TOPPING
3 egg whites
Pinch of salt
¼ cup sugar
A few teaspoons of sugar for dusting

1. Prepare the lemon cream. In the top of a double boiler, mix sugar, flour, and salt together. Add lemon juice and rind. Mix well. Beat in water, egg yolks, and butter (if the butter is still chunky it will melt over the hot water).

2. Place mixture over hot simmering water in a double boiler and cook until smooth and thick, stirring constantly with a whisk (about 20 minutes). Cool and set aside. Preheat oven to 350°F.

3. Mix flour, baking powder, salt, and lemon rind together. Set aside.

4. Cream butter and sugar together until light and fluffy. Add eggs, one at a time, beating after each addition. Add lemon juice and beat until well blended. Add flour mixture and continue beating until batter is smooth.

5. Fill 12 cupcake papers with the batter. Cook for 15 minutes or until cupcakes are golden on top. Remove from oven and cool for 10 minutes.

6. To make the meringue: beat egg whites with a pinch of salt until they start to stiffen. Gradually add sugar, beating until stiff but not dry.

7. Using a sharp knife, carefully remove a little cone from the center of the cooled cupcakes using an apple corer and fill with lemon cream.

8. Place 1 tablespoon meringue on each cupcake, forming peaks with the back of a spoon or a fork. Dust lightly with sugar. Cook cupcakes in the oven for another 5–7 minutes or until meringue is just golden. Let cool.

# APPLE-CRANBERRY CRUMBLE Cupcakes

These moist cupcakes will remind you of the homemade crumbles you ate when you were a kid. The cranberries give a slightly tart taste and a beautiful color.

**MAKES: ABOUT 18 CUPCAKES**

1½ cups all-purpose flour
2 teaspoons baking powder
1 teaspoon salt
2 teaspoons cinnamon
½ teaspoon grated nutmeg
¾ cup/1½ sticks unsalted butter, room temperature
1½ cups sugar
2 eggs
1 cup applesauce (you can either use ready-made or recipe on page 134)
1 tablespoon finely grated lemon rind
1 cup cranberries (fresh or frozen)
½ cup walnuts, chopped (optional)

APPLE-WALNUT CRUMBLE TOPPING
2 tablespoons/¼ stick unsalted butter
6 teaspoons sugar
⅓ cup all-purpose flour
1 apple, peeled and cut into small pieces
½ cup walnuts, chopped

1. Preheat oven to 350°F.

2. Mix dry ingredients and spices together and set aside.

3. In the large bowl of an electric mixer, cream butter and sugar until light and fluffy. Add eggs, one at a time, beating well after each addition. Alternately add dry ingredients, applesauce, and lemon rind and blend well. Fold in cranberries and walnuts, if desired. If you are using frozen cranberries, don't defrost them beforehand.

4. Spoon batter into cupcake papers, filling cups a little over ½ full. Smooth batter with the back of a spoon.

5. For topping, melt butter in a pan, add sugar, flour, apple, and walnuts. Mix well and stir until mixture just starts to change color. Remove from heat. Place a spoonful of the mixture on top of each cupcake. Cook cupcakes for about 20 minutes or until a tester inserted into the center comes out clean. Remove from oven and cool completely before removing cupcakes from tin.

**CUPCAKE TIP**
*Serve these cupcakes with a dollop of whipped cream on top.*

# MAPLE WALNUT DELIGHTS

These cupcakes are a true gourmet delight. The icing is a good example of cooked frosting at its best—it is both beautiful to look at and will melt in your mouth.

**MAKES: ABOUT 18 CUPCAKES**

2 ½ cups all-purpose flour
3 teaspoons baking powder
½ teaspoon salt
½ cup/1 stick unsalted butter, room temperature
½ cup light brown sugar
2 eggs
1 cup maple syrup
½ cup milk
½ cup chopped walnuts

MAPLE MERINGUE ICING
2 egg whites
Pinch of salt
1 cup maple syrup
1 teaspoon vanilla extract
½ cup chopped walnuts or walnut halves (for decoration)

1. Preheat oven to 350°F.

2. Mix flour, baking powder, and salt together and set aside.

3. In the large bowl of an electric mixer, cream butter and sugar until light and fluffy. Add eggs, one at a time, mixing well after each addition. Alternately add dry ingredients and syrup and milk, blending well after each addition. Fold in walnuts.

4. Spoon batter into cupcake papers, filling cups about ⅔ full. Bake for 25–30 minutes or until a tester inserted into the center comes out clean. Remove from oven and cool.

5. To make the icing: beat egg whites with a pinch of salt until peaks start to form. Set aside.

6. Boil maple syrup until it forms a soft ball when dropped into a glass of water (about 234°F on a candy thermometer). The time will depend on the maple syrup you are using but should be about 5–10 minutes. Remove from heat immediately. Slowly pour the hot syrup into the egg whites, beating constantly. The hot syrup actually cooks the egg whites. Add vanilla and continue beating until mixture is stiff and stands in soft peaks.

7. Ice the cooled cupcakes, forming peaks with the back of a spoon or a fork. Place a walnut half on top of each cupcake or sprinkle with chopped walnuts before icing hardens. It will harden on the outside and remain soft and creamy inside.

# THREE-GINGERBREAD
## Cupcakes

The fresh and crystallized ginger give these cupcakes a unique and very pronounced flavor. Enjoy with a cup of strong black tea or an espresso.

**MAKES: ABOUT 12 CUPCAKES**

1½ cups all-purpose flour
2 teaspoons baking powder
1 teaspoon salt
1 teaspoon ground ginger
½ teaspoon cinnamon
½ teaspoon allspice
Dash each of grated nutmeg and
    ground cloves
½ cup/1 stick unsalted butter, room
    temperature
¾ cup brown sugar
2 eggs
1 teaspoon vanilla extract
1 heaping tablespoon grated ginger
½ cup milk
3 tablespoons finely chopped
    crystallized ginger

FROSTING
1 cup whipping cream, chilled
4 tablespoons sugar
½ teaspoon ground ginger
1 teaspoon finely grated fresh ginger
Sliced crystallized ginger for decoration

1. Preheat oven to 350°F.

2. Mix flour, baking powder, salt, and spices together and set aside.

3. In the large bowl of an electric mixer, cream butter and sugar until light and fluffy. Add eggs, one at a time, mixing well after each addition. Add vanilla and grated ginger. Alternately add dry ingredients and milk, beating continually. When batter is smooth, fold in crystallized ginger.

4. Spoon batter into cupcake papers, filling cups about ⅔ full. Bake for 20–25 minutes or until a tester inserted in the center comes out clean. Remove from oven and cool.

5. To make the frosting: whip cream with an electric beater until almost stiff. Gradually add sugar and ground ginger, beating constantly, until stiff peaks form. Fold in grated fresh ginger and frost cooled cupcakes. Sprinkle with ground ginger (go easy!) and decorate with a slice of crystallized ginger. These cupcakes have to be frosted just before serving them. They will not keep for long unless you use some sort of fixative for the whipped cream.

**CUPCAKE TIP**
*Alternatively, make a simple glaze by heating a few tablespoons of ginger preserves.*

# STRAWBERRY-FILLED OATMEAL Cupcakes

These moist and crunchy cupcakes make a delicious dessert or a welcome snack, and if they aren't all gobbled down immediately, they keep well and can be eaten for breakfast.

MAKES: **ABOUT 12 CUPCAKES**

1 cup all-purpose flour
1 teaspoon baking powder
1 teaspoon baking soda
1 teaspoon salt
1 teaspoon cinnamon
³/₄ cup rolled oats
¹/₂ cup/1 stick unsalted butter,
   room temperature
³/₄ cup sugar
1 egg
1 teaspoon vanilla extract
1 cup sour cream
12 teaspoons strawberry jelly

OATMEAL CRUNCH TOPPING
¹/₂ cup rolled oats
¹/₄ cup light brown sugar
2 heaping tablespoons all-purpose
   flour
1 teaspoon cinnamon
¹/₂ teaspoon salt
¹/₄ cup/¹/₂ stick unsalted butter,
   chilled and cut into little pieces

1. Put all of the topping ingredients in a food processor and process until lumps form. Set aside.

2. Preheat oven to 350°F.

3. Mix dry ingredients together and set aside.

4. In the large bowl of an electric mixer, cream butter and sugar until light and fluffy. Add egg and vanilla and mix well. Alternately add dry ingredients and sour cream, blending well after each addition.

5. Spoon half of the batter into 12 cupcake papers. Make an indentation and place 1 teaspoon of jelly in each cupcake. Fill cupcakes with remaining batter. Using your fingers, sprinkle a little topping over each cupcake. Cook for 25–30 minutes or until cupcakes are golden brown on top. Remove from oven and cool.

**CUPCAKE TIP**
*Any type of jelly
can be used for
the filling.*

# PERSIMMON NUT HARVEST Treats

These cupcakes are a nice alternative to spice cake and a good way to use persimmons.

**MAKES: ABOUT 18 CUPCAKES**

1¾ cups all-purpose flour
2 teaspoons baking powder
1 teaspoon salt
1 teaspoon cinnamon
½ teaspoon ground ginger
Dash each of grated nutmeg and
    ground cloves
1 tablespoon grated orange rind
1 cup/2 sticks unsalted butter
¾ cup granulated white sugar
¾ cup light brown sugar
1 egg
1 cup puréed persimmon pulp (about
    3 very ripe persimmons)
1 cup coarsely ground nuts (walnuts,
    pecans, or hazelnuts)

ORANGE CREAM CHEESE FROSTING
1 cup cream cheese
2 tablespoons/¼ stick unsalted butter
1½ cups powdered sugar
1 teaspoon grated orange rind
2 teaspoons orange juice
Dried persimmons for decoration

1. Preheat oven to 350°F.

2. Mix all of the dry ingredients together and stir in the orange rind. Set aside.

3. In the large bowl of an electric mixer, cream butter and sugars until light and fluffy. Add egg and beat well. Alternately add flour mixture and persimmon pulp, beating well after each addition. Fold in nuts.

4. Spoon batter into cupcake papers, filling cups about ⅔ full. Smooth batter with the back of a spoon. Bake for 25 minutes or until a tester inserted into the center comes out clean. Remove from oven and cool completely before unmolding.

5. To make the frosting: in a large bowl, cream together cream cheese and butter until smooth and well blended. Gradually add sugar and beat until the mixture is light and fluffy. Beat in the orange rind and juice and place in the refrigerator for about an hour before frosting cooled cupcakes. Top with a piece of dried persimmon.

**CUPCAKE TIP**
*You can substitute lemon for the orange in both the cupcake and the frosting.*

# STRAWBERRY RHUBARB CRISP Cupcakes

Strawberries and rhubarb go particularly well together. The strawberries seem to bring out the subtle flavor of the rhubarb as well as its color.

**MAKES: ABOUT 16 REGULAR CUPCAKES OR 8 JUMBO CUPCAKES**

1 cup chopped rhubarb, fresh or frozen

1 cup sugar, plus 3 tablespoons if you are using fresh rhubarb (see step 1)

2 cups all-purpose flour

2 teaspoons baking powder

1 teaspoon baking soda

1 teaspoon salt

1 teaspoon cinnamon

1/2 cup/1 stick unsalted butter, room temperature

2 eggs

1 teaspoon vanilla extract

1 cup buttermilk (you can substitute milk, in which case you eliminate the baking soda)

STRAWBERRY GLAZE

1/2 cup strawberry jelly

1 cup fresh strawberries, washed, cleaned, and cut into quarters lengthwise, for decoration

1. If you are using fresh rhubarb, wash and peel the rhubarb, cut it into small slices (as you would celery) and place it in a colander in the sink or over a bowl. Sprinkle with 3 tablespoons sugar and let drain for half an hour. This will make the rhubarb more tender and will bring out its taste.

2. Preheat oven to 350°F.

3. Mix flour, baking powder, baking soda, salt, and cinnamon together and set aside.

4. In the large bowl of an electric mixer, cream butter and sugar until light and fluffy. Add eggs, one at a time, mixing well after each addition. Add vanilla. Alternately add dry ingredients and buttermilk or milk, beating continually. When batter is smooth, fold in rhubarb.

5. Spoon batter into either regular or jumbo cupcake papers, filling about 2/3 full. Bake for 20–25 minutes or until a tester inserted into the center comes out clean. Remove from oven and cool.

6. Melt strawberry jelly over very low heat. When just melted, spread on cooled cupcakes with a pastry brush. Place sliced strawberries in a circle in the center. Brush a little jelly over them so that they will stay in place and take on a glossy sheen.

# ȢOGURT Cupcakes

These very-easy-to-make cupcakes are both healthy and tasty and will make a great snack or an elegant dessert, accompanied by a fresh fruit salad.

**MAKES: ABOUT 18 CUPCAKES**

1 container yogurt (about ½ cup)
2 containers sugar
3 eggs, lightly beaten
½ container vegetable oil
3 containers all-purpose flour
2 teaspoons baking powder
1 teaspoon salt
Flavoring (vanilla, almond extract, etc.—see step 3)

**CUPCAKE TIP**
*The yogurt container will be your measuring cup—so no mess!*

1. Preheat oven to 350°F.

2. In a large bowl, mix the yogurt, sugar, and eggs until completely blended with a whisk or a wooden spoon. Add oil and stir. Add flour, baking powder, and salt and beat until smooth.

3. Add the flavoring of your choice—you could add ½ cup fresh, dried, or candied fruit or nuts. You can also add the flavoring extract of your choice—vanilla, almond, mint, lemon (with a little grated lemon rind), orange flower water, etc. Or you can add food coloring to make party or holiday cupcakes. Divide up the batter and make several different colors.

4. Spoon batter into cupcake papers, filling cups about ⅔ full. Cook cupcakes for about 25 minutes or until a tester inserted into the center comes out clean. Remove from oven and cool.

VARIATION: FRUIT ȢOGURT CUPCAKES

Use the basic recipe above but instead of plain yogurt, use one with fruit or other ingredients already added.

★ If you are using a berry yogurt, add ½ cup dried, frozen, or fresh fruit, cut into small pieces, or a tablespoon of kirsch or fruit liquor.

★ If you are using apricot yogurt, add 2 tablespoons ground almonds, top the cooked cupcakes with apricot glaze and caramelized almonds.

★ If you are using strawberry or raspberry yogurt, top cooked cupcakes with whipped cream with added chopped fresh fruit.

# POPPYSEED & LAVENDER HONEY Cupcakes

Cooking the poppyseeds in honey gives the cupcakes a distinctive flavor.
I prefer lavender honey but you can use the honey of your choice.

**MAKES: ABOUT 24 REGULAR
CUPCAKES OR 12 JUMBO
CUPCAKES**

1 cup poppyseeds
$\frac{1}{2}$ cup honey
$\frac{1}{4}$ cup water
2$\frac{1}{2}$ cups all-purpose flour
1 teaspoon baking soda
1 teaspoon salt, plus a good pinch for
   egg whites
1 cup/2 sticks unsalted butter, room
   temperature
1$\frac{1}{2}$ cups sugar
4 eggs, separated
1 teaspoon vanilla extract
1 cup sour cream (you can use
   whipping or liquid cream instead)
Powdered sugar for dusting

1. Preheat oven to 350°F. Cook the poppyseeds with honey and water for about 5 minutes. Let cool.

2. Mix flour, baking soda, and salt together and set aside.

3. In the bowl of an electric mixer, cream butter with sugar until light and fluffy. Add cooled poppyseed mixture. Blend well. Add egg yolks, one at a time, beating well after each addition. Blend in vanilla and sour cream. Add dry ingredients to mixture, blending well.

4. Beat egg whites with a good pinch of salt until stiff but not dry. Gently fold into batter.

5. Spoon batter into either regular or jumbo cupcake papers, filling cups just a little over $\frac{1}{2}$ full. Cook for about 15 minutes or until golden brown on top. Cooking time will depend on the size of the cupcakes you are making. Loosely cover cupcakes with a piece of aluminum foil and cook for another 5–10 minutes or until a tester comes out clean. Remove from oven and cool. Dust with powdered sugar.

# SUNSHINE & VITAMIN C
## Cupcakes

Just what Grandma ordered! Besides being lovely to look at, these cupcakes provide a triple dose of vitamin C with the lemon, orange, and grapefruit juices.

MAKES: **ABOUT 16 CUPCAKES**

2 cups all-purpose flour
2 teaspoons baking powder
1 teaspoon salt
1 teaspoon each finely grated lemon, orange, and grapefruit rind
1/2 cup/1 stick unsalted butter, room temperature
1 1/4 cups sugar
2 eggs
2/3 cup orange and grapefruit juice mixed (preferably in equal parts)
1 tablespoon lemon juice

THREE CITRUS FRUIT CUSTARD
3 tablespoons each of lemon juice, orange juice, and grapefruit juice
1/3 cup water
1/2 cup sugar
2 tablespoons all purpose flour
Pinch of salt
3 egg yolks (or 1 egg and 1 yolk)
Candied or jellied citrus fruit for decoration

1. Preheat oven to 350°F.

2. Mix flour, baking powder, and salt together in a medium bowl. Add the fruit rinds and set aside.

3. In the large bowl of an electric mixer, cream butter and sugar until light and fluffy. Add eggs, one at a time, mixing well after each addition. Alternately add dry ingredients and fruit juices, blending until smooth.

4. Fill cupcake papers about 2/3 full. Bake for about 25 minutes or until a tester inserted into the center comes out clean. Remove from oven and cool.

5. Mix all the custard ingredients together in a large bowl over simmering water. Stir mixture constantly until it is hot to the touch and thick. It should coat the back of a wooden spoon.

6. Remove from heat and cool, stirring from time to time so that a skin doesn't form. When it has cooled, you can cover it with plastic wrap and put it in the refrigerator until you are ready to use it. Heap onto cooled cupcakes and top with a piece of candied or jellied citrus fruit.

**CUPCAKE TIP**
*You can also cut the center out of the cupcakes and fill it with a heaping portion of custard.*

# KIDS'
## CUPCAKES

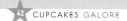 

# YETI Cupcakes

The Yeti, or the Abominable Snowman, is a mythical creature. The only thing that everyone agrees on about Yeti is that he is snow white—and very cool. Thus, the Yeti Cupcake!

**MAKES: ABOUT 18 CUPCAKES**

WHITE VELVET CUPCAKE
2 cups all-purpose flour
2 teaspoons baking power
1 teaspoon salt, plus a pinch for the egg whites
½ cup/1 stick unsalted butter, room temperature
1¼ cups sugar
⅔ cup milk
1 teaspoon vanilla extract (you can replace with another flavoring if you prefer: lemon, almond extract, etc.)
3 egg whites
1 cup mini-marshmallows

SNOW FROSTING
2 egg whites
¾ cup sugar
¼ cup light corn syrup
Pinch of salt
1 teaspoon vanilla extract
½ cup sweetened shredded coconut (optional)
Sweetened shredded coconut for decoration

1. Preheat oven to 350°F.

2. Mix flour, baking powder, and salt together and set aside.

3. Cream butter and sugar until light and fluffy. Alternately add flour mixture and milk and beat until batter is smooth. Add flavoring.

4. Beat egg whites with a pinch of salt until stiff but not dry. Gently fold into batter. Fold in mini-marshmallows.

5. Spoon batter into cupcake papers, filling cups about ⅔ full. Bake for 20–25 minutes or until tester inserted into the center comes out clean. Remove from oven and cool.

6. To make the frosting: in a large bowl, preferably the top of a double boiler, mix egg whites, sugar, corn syrup, and salt until combined. Place the bowl over simmering water and whisk until the sugar dissolves and the mixture is hot. This will take about 3 minutes. Remove from heat and beat for 5–7 minutes until frosting is cool and stiff peaks form. Beat in vanilla and delicately fold in the coconut by hand, if desired. The frosting will be ready to spread. Decorate frosted cupcakes to your taste.

**CUPCAKE TIP**
*This is one version of what is know as a "7-minute frosting." It is light and delicious and has a marshmallow feel to it.*

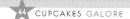 

# CHOCOLATE HAZELNUT
## Cupcakes with Chocolate Hazelnut Spread

Chocolate hazelnut spreads are a great favorite among French children (and adults!) on a fresh baguette or a hot crepe for breakfast or a snack. These light cupcakes will be a big success for any kid's birthday party or a special dessert for the whole family.

**MAKES: ABOUT 16 CUPCAKES**

1³/₄ cups all-purpose flour

2 teaspoons baking powder

¹/₂ teaspoon salt

¹/₂ cup/1 stick unsalted butter, room temperature

¹/₂ cup sugar

3 eggs

1¹/₂ cups chocolate hazelnut spread (Nutella or similar)

¹/₄ cup milk

¹/₂ cup roasted ground hazelnuts or whole hazelnuts for topping (optional)

1. Preheat oven to 350°F.

2. Mix flour, baking powder, and salt together and set aside.

3. Cream butter and sugar until light and fluffy. Add eggs, one at a time, mixing well after each addition. Add half of the chocolate hazelnut spread and blend thoroughly. Alternately add flour mixture and milk, blending well after each addition.

4. Spoon batter into cupcake papers, filling about ²/₃ full. Bake for 20–25 minutes or until a tester inserted into the center comes out clean. Remove from oven and cool.

5. When cupcakes are cool, generously frost them with remaining chocolate hazelnut spread. Sprinkle with roasted ground hazelnuts or place a whole or half hazelnut on top of each cupcake.

# ROOT BEER Floats

Root beer floats were a staple of my childhood and teenage years and the mere thought brings back memories of hot summers where I grew up. My parents used to take us to the ice cream parlor where we could indulge in what seemed at the time like a mile-high root beer float. Try one of these on a warm summer day and see if it has the same effect on you!

**MAKES: ABOUT 16 CUPCAKES**

1 cup all-purpose flour
1 cup sugar
1 teaspoon baking powder
1 teaspoon baking soda
1 teaspoon salt
$\frac{1}{2}$ cup root beer
$\frac{1}{2}$ cup/1 stick unsalted butter, cut
　　into small pieces
1 egg, slightly beaten
$\frac{1}{3}$ cup buttermilk
1 teaspoon vanilla extract
1 cup mini-marshmallows (optional)
ROOT BEER FROSTING
2 cups powdered sugar
Pinch of salt
$\frac{1}{4}$ cup root beer
$\frac{1}{2}$ cup/1 stick unsalted butter, cut
　　into small pieces
1 teaspoon vanilla extract
Whipped cream for topping
Root beer candies (optional) for
　　decoration
Decorative straws

1. Preheat oven to 350°F.

2. In a large bowl, mix flour, sugar, baking powder, baking soda, and salt together and set aside.

3. In a heavy pan, bring root beer and butter to a boil, stirring constantly. Remove from heat and pour into flour mixture, beating well with a wooden spoon. Add egg, buttermilk, and vanilla. When batter is smooth, fold in mini-marshmallows.

4. Spoon batter into cupcake papers, filling cups about $\frac{2}{3}$ full. Bake for 20–25 minutes or until a tester inserted into the center comes out clean. Remove from oven and cool.

5. To make the frosting: place powdered sugar and salt in a large bowl.

6. In a heavy pan, bring root beer and butter to a boil, stirring constantly. Remove from heat and slowly add to sugar, stirring continually until mixture is smooth. When frosting has cooled, beat it for a few minutes with an electric beater. Frost cupcakes and top each cupcake with a dab of whipped cream and a root beer candy, if desired. Cut pretty straws in half and stick one into each cupcake.

# BIRTHDAY Beauties

You can of course use any recipe for a birthday cake but I have suggested three here that are sure to please the kids—strawberry, lemon, and chocolate. My mother used to make these for my birthday parties when I was little and ice them with lovely pastel-colored frosting.

**MAKES: ABOUT 12 CUPCAKES**

STRAWBERRY CUPCAKE
2¹/₂ cups all-purpose flour
³/₄ cup sugar
2¹/₂ teaspoons baking powder
1 teaspoon baking soda
¹/₂ teaspoon salt
1 cup buttermilk
6 tablespoons/³/₄ stick unsalted
    butter, melted and slightly cooled
2 eggs, slightly beaten
1 teaspoon vanilla extract
1 cup fresh strawberries, cleaned and
    cut into small pieces

PASTEL CUPCAKE FROSTING
1 x quantity ready-to-use fondant
    frosting (about 1 cup per
    12 cupcakes)
Food coloring (various colors)

FOR DECORATION
Shredded coconut
Chocolate sprinkles
Candies
Colored sugars
Candied fruits
Nuts

1. Preheat oven to 350°F. In a large bowl, mix flour, sugar, baking powder, baking soda, and salt together and set aside.

2. In another bowl, mix buttermilk, melted butter, eggs, and vanilla. Add liquid ingredients to dry ingredients and beat well with a wooden spoon. Fold in strawberries.

3. Spoon batter into cupcake papers, filling cups about ²/₃ full. Bake for 20–25 minutes or until a tester inserted into the center comes out clean. Remove from oven and cool.

4. To make the pastel frosting: put fondant frosting in separate bowls and add several drops of food coloring to each bowl until you obtain the desired color. Frost or dip cupcakes in frosting and decorate with shredded coconut, chocolate sprinkles, little candies, colored sugars, candied fruits, nuts, etc.

VARIATION: LEMON CUPCAKES

Follow recipe for Easter Lemon Chiffon Cupcakes (page 126) and top with the pastel cupcake frosting. Decorate as desired.

VARIATION: CHOCOLATE CUPCAKES

Follow any of the chocolate cupcake recipes in this book, such as Chocolate Hazelnut Cupcake (page 44) or Chocolate Malted Milkshake Cupcake (page 58). Decorate as desired.

# CHOCOLATE SUNDAE Cupcakes

These one-egg cupcakes will be light and velvety and the vanilla bean will give them an unrivaled flavor.

**MAKES: ABOUT 18 CUPCAKES**

REAL VANILLA CUPCAKE

¾ cup milk

1 vanilla bean, split lengthwise

2 cups all-purpose flour

2 teaspoons baking powder

1 teaspoon salt

½ cup/1 stick unsalted butter, room temperature

1 cup sugar

1 egg

OLD-FASHIONED FUDGE FROSTING

1½ cups sugar

¾ cup milk

2 tablespoons unsweetened cocoa powder

Pinch of salt

1 tablespoon unsalted butter

1 teaspoon vanilla extract

½ cup finely ground peanuts (optional)

Maraschino cherries for decoration

1. In a small saucepan, heat milk with vanilla bean. When milk boils, remove from heat immediately and let cool, about an hour. After the milk has cooled, remove the vanilla bean and scrape out the inside into the milk Discard the bean.

2. Preheat oven to 350°F. Mix flour, baking powder, and salt together and set aside.

3. Cream butter and sugar until light and fluffy. Add egg and beat well. Alternately add dry ingredients and milk, mixing well after each addition.

4. Spoon batter into cupcake papers, filling cups about ⅔ full. Bake for about 15–20 minutes or until a tester inserted into the center comes out clean. Remove from oven and cool.

5. To make the frosting: mix sugar, milk, cocoa, and salt in a medium pan. Cook slowly over medium heat until mixture comes to a boil. Continue cooking until mixture forms a soft ball when dropped into a glass of water (about 234°F on a candy thermometer). This may take 15 minutes. Remove mixture from heat. Add butter and vanilla and blend well.

6. Put pan in cold water and beat until mixture is of spreading consistency. This could take 15 minutes. Spread on cupcakes immediately, sprinkle with peanuts, if desired, and top with a cherry before the frosting hardens.

# COOKIES 'N' CREAM
## Cupcakes

Remember when you were a kid and you used to dunk those cookies in a tall glass of cold milk? Well, this is the cupcake version. Use any type of sandwich cookie—choose your favorite.

**MAKES: ABOUT 18–20 CUPCAKES**

1²/₃ cups all-purpose flour
2 teaspoons baking powder
1 teaspoon salt
¹/₂ cup/1 stick unsalted butter, room
   temperature
1 cup sugar
2 eggs
1 teaspoon vanilla extract
³/₄ cup half-and-half or light cream
1 cup coarsely crushed sandwich
   cookies (Oreo type)

WHITE CHOCOLATE
CREAM CHEESE FROSTING
6 ounces good quality white
   chocolate, broken into pieces
³/₄ cup cream cheese, softened, cut
   into pieces
6 tablespoons/³/₄ stick unsalted
   butter, room temperature,
   cut into pieces
Miniature sandwich cookies or
   crushed cookies for decoration

1. Preheat oven to 350°F.

2. Mix flour, baking powder, and salt together and set aside.

3. Cream butter and sugar until light and fluffy. Add eggs, one at a time, mixing well after each addition. Add vanilla. Alternately add flour mixture and half-and-half or cream and beat until batter is smooth. Fold in crushed cookies.

4. Spoon batter into cupcake papers, filling cups about ²/₃ full. Bake for 20–25 minutes or until a tester inserted into the center comes out clean. Remove from oven and cool.

5. To make the frosting: in a microwave or a double boiler, melt white chocolate until smooth and creamy, just a few minutes. It should be just warm to the touch.

6. Beat the cream cheese and butter until light and fluffy. Add melted chocolate and beat again until smooth. Use the frosting immediately or it will harden. Press in a little cookie or sprinkle with crushed cookies at once, while frosting is still soft. This frosting looks like the cream filling in sandwich cookies.

# HOT CHOCOLATE & MARSHMALLOW
## Cupcakes

Serve these delicious chocolate cupcakes while they are still warm to get the full effect.

**MAKES: ABOUT 12 CUPCAKES**

8 ounces dark chocolate
1 cup/2 sticks unsalted butter, room
   temperature
4 eggs
1 cup sugar
¾ cup all-purpose flour
1 teaspoon salt
½ cup mini-chocolate chips or grated
   chocolate
Marshmallows or mini-marshmallows
   for decoration

1. Preheat oven to 350°F. Melt chocolate and butter in a double boiler or microwave until just melted (do not cook). Set aside until just warm.

3. Cream the eggs and sugar together until light and foamy. Add flour and salt and mix. Pour in the chocolate mixture and beat until batter is smooth.

4. Spoon batter into 12 cupcake papers. Sprinkle a scant teaspoon of mini-chocolate chips or grated chocolate over each cupcake and bake for 15 minutes. Remove cupcakes from oven. They will be very moist inside.

5. Place a marshmallow or several mini-marshmallows on each cupcake. Put cupcakes under broiler for a few seconds until marshmallows start to brown. This will take only a second so be very careful. Remove from oven and wait for about 5 minutes before eating since the marshmallows will be very hot. These cupcakes are best eaten while still slightly warm.

**CUPCAKE TIP**
*Alternatively, bake in a silicon mold. Leave off the marshmallow and sprinkle with a few grains of "fleur de sel."*

# JELLY-FILLED Cupcakes

These cupcakes are perfect for any occasion and can be decorated accordingly for birthdays or holidays or for a special dessert or snack.

**MAKES: ABOUT 12 CUPCAKES**

BASIC YELLOW CUPCAKE
1½ cups all-purpose flour
2 teaspoons baking powder
1 teaspoon salt
½ cup/1 stick unsalted butter, room temperature
1 cup sugar
2 eggs
1 teaspoon vanilla extract (or another flavoring, such as almond extract, orange flower water, etc.)
½ cup milk
Jam, jelly, marmalade, or preserves of your choice

BASIC WHITE CUPCAKE ICING
3 tbsp hot milk or cream
2½ cups powdered sugar

FOR DECORATION
Colored sugars
Candies
Stencils etc.

1. Preheat oven to 350°F. Mix dry ingredients together and set aside.

2. Cream butter and sugar until light and fluffy. Add eggs, one at a time, mixing well after each addition. Add vanilla. Alternately add flour mixture and milk and beat until batter is smooth.

3. Spoon batter into cupcake papers, filling cups about ⅔ full. Bake for 20–25 minutes or until tester inserted into the center comes out clean. Remove from oven and cool.

4. When cupcakes are cool, scoop out the center and fill with the jam, jelly, marmalade, or preserves of your choice. Replace the core.

5. Put hot milk or cream in a large bowl. Gradually add sugar until icing is thick enough to spread. Beat for several minutes until icing is smooth and creamy. You may need to add more sugar or liquid to get the right consistency but remember to beat well after each addition.

6. While the icing is still soft, decorate with colored sugars, candies, stencils, etc.

VARIATION: BASIC CHOCOLATE CUPCAKE

Use the recipe for Basic Yellow Cupcake but replace ¼ cup flour with ¼ cup unsweetened cocoa powder.

VARIATION: BASIC CHOCOLATE CUPCAKE ICING

Use the recipe for Basic White Cupcake Icing but replace ¼ cup powdered sugar with ¼ cup unsweetened cocoa powder.

# PEANUT BUTTER & JELLY SWIRLS

These cupcakes are definitely a throwback to childhood and those peanut butter and jelly sandwiches of my youth.

**MAKES: ABOUT 20 CUPCAKES**

2½ cups all-purpose flour
3 teaspoons baking powder
1 teaspoon salt
½ cup/1 stick unsalted butter, room temperature
1½ cups light brown sugar
¾ cup chunky peanut butter
1 teaspoon vanilla extract
3 eggs
1 cup half-and-half or light cream
4 ounces jelly (about 6 heaping tablespoons)

PEANUT BUTTER FROSTING
¼ cup/½ stick unsalted butter, room temperature
½ cup smooth peanut butter
2 cups powdered sugar
2 tablespoons milk

FOR DECORATION
½ cup chopped peanuts
Jelly

1. Preheat oven to 350°F.

2. Mix flour, baking powder, and salt together and set aside.

3. Cream butter and sugar until light and fluffy. Add peanut butter and vanilla and continue beating until thoroughly blended.Add eggs, one at a time, mixing well after each addition. Alternately add half-and-half or cream and dry ingredients, beating well after each addition.

4. Dollop the jelly over the cupcake batter in 6 heaping tablespoons. Swirl jelly into batter with a long knife or spatula. Don't overmix.

5. Spoon batter into cupcake papers, filling cups about ⅔ full. Bake for 25–30 minutes or until a tester inserted in the center comes out clean. Remove from oven and cool.

6. Make the frosting: cream butter, peanut butter, and sugar together until light and fluffy. Gradually add milk and beat until creamy and of spreading consistency. You can add more milk if needed.

7. Ice cupcakes, add a swirl of jelly, and sprinkle with chopped peanuts.

**CUPCAKE TIP**
*You can also fill the cupcake with jelly rather than swirling it in—just take out the center of a cooled cupcake with an apple core, put a teaspoon of jelly in the hole and replace the core.*

# ROCKY ROAD
## Cupcakes

Rocky Road is a big favorite among kids. It is usually a combination of chocolate, walnuts, marshmallows, and chocolate chips, whether it be in an ice cream, a brownie, or a cupcake. You can improvise with this recipe—tailor it to your family's and friends' tastes.

**MAKES: ABOUT 18 CUPCAKES**

1½ cups all-purpose flour
2 teaspoons baking powder
1 teaspoon salt
⅓ cup unsweetened cocoa powder
4 ounces dark chocolate
¼ cup vegetable oil
1 egg
1 teaspoon vanilla extract
1 cup milk
½ cup mini-marshmallows
½ cup dark chocolate chips,
   plus ½ cup for topping
½ cup coarsely chopped walnuts,
   plus ½ cup for topping
½ cup white chocolate chips for
   topping (optional)

1. Preheat oven to 350°F.

2. Mix flour, baking powder, salt, and cocoa powder together, mix thoroughly, and set aside.

3. Melt chocolate in a microwave or a double boiler (do not cook). Remove from heat as soon as chocolate is just melted. Using either an electric mixer or a wooden spoon, beat in oil, egg, and vanilla. Alternately add flour mixture and milk, beating well after each addition. When batter is smooth and thoroughly blended, fold in ½ cup each mini-marshmallows, chocolate chips, and walnuts.

4. Spoon batter into cupcake papers, filling just over ½ full. Mix remaining walnuts and chocolate chips together and sprinkle over batter. Bake for about 20 minutes or until topping is cooked. If the topping starts to burn before the cupcakes are cooked, cover lightly with a piece of aluminum foil. Remove from oven and cool.

**CUPCAKE TIP**
*Try using
different flavor chips
(mint, peanut,
coffee, etc.)*

# BANANA SPLIT
## Cupcakes

Who doesn't remember banana splits from their childhood, when no one worried about their waistlines or cholesterol level!

**MAKES: ABOUT 18 CUPCAKES**

2 cups all-purpose flour
2 teaspoons baking powder
1 teaspoon baking soda
1 teaspoon salt
½ cup/1 stick unsalted butter
1½ cups sugar
2 eggs
1 teaspoon vanilla extract
1 cup ripe mashed bananas (about
   2 medium bananas)
½ cup buttermilk or sour cream
Strawberry preserves for filling
CHOCOLATE FUDGE ICING
4 tablespoons/¼ stick unsalted
   butter, cut into little pieces
4 ounces dark chocolate, broken
   into pieces
3 cups powdered sugar
⅓ cup hot milk
1 teaspoon vanilla extract
Pinch of salt
Maraschino cherries and banana
   candies for decoration

1. Preheat oven to 350°F.

2. Mix flour, baking powder, baking soda, and salt together and set aside.

3. Cream butter and sugar until light and fluffy. Add eggs, one at a time, mixing well after each addition. Add vanilla and mashed bananas and mix thoroughly. Alternately beat in flour mixture and liquid and blend until smooth.

4. Spoon batter into cupcake papers, filling cups about ⅔ full. Smooth batter with the back of a spoon. Bake for 20 minutes or until a tester inserted in the center comes out clean. Remove from oven and cool.

5. When cupcakes are cool, scoop out the center of each cupcake with an apple corer. Drop in a teaspoon of strawberry preserves.

6. To make the icing: melt butter and chocolate in a double boiler or a microwave. Stir until just melted and set aside until cool to the touch. You can set the bowl in cold water to speed up the process.

7. Put sugar and hot milk in a large bowl and stir until smooth. Add vanilla, salt, and chocolate mixture. Using an electric beater, beat icing until smooth and thickened, about 5 minutes. Ice cooled, filled cupcakes. Decorate with a cherry and banana candies.

# S'MORES
## Cupcakes

I guess that anyone who grew up in the United States knows what a S'more is—
a sort of graham cracker sandwich with chocolate and marshmallow. Here is my
cupcake version. I hope you will find it to your liking and will ask for s'more!

MAKES: **ABOUT 18 CUPCAKES**

GRAHAM CRACKER AND MILK
CHOCOLATE CUPCAKE
½ cup all-purpose flour
1½ cups finely crushed graham
   crackers (about 20 grahams)
2 teaspoons baking powder
1 teaspoon salt
½ cup/1 stick unsalted butter, room
   temperature
¾ cup sugar
2 eggs
1 teaspoon vanilla extract
¾ cup milk
1 cup milk chocolate chips
NO-COOK MARSHMALLOW ICING
2 egg whites
Pinch of salt or ¼ teaspoon cream of
   tartar
¼ cup sugar
¾ cup corn syrup
Grated milk chocolate or chocolate
   sprinkles for decoration

1. Preheat oven to 350°F.

2. Mix flour, crushed graham crackers, baking powder, and salt together
and set aside.

3. Cream butter and sugar until light and fluffy. Add eggs, one at a time,
mixing well after each addition. Add vanilla. Alternately add flour mixture
and milk and beat until batter is smooth. Fold in chocolate chips.

4. Spoon batter into cupcake papers, filling cups about ⅔ full. Bake for
20–25 minutes or until a tester inserted into the center comes out clean.
Remove from oven and cool.

5. To make the icing: beat egg whites with salt or cream of tartar until soft
peaks form. Gradually add sugar, beating continually. Slowly add
corn syrup. Icing will form peaks and will have a marshmallow
consistency. Ice cooled cupcakes and sprinkle with milk chocolate or
chocolate sprinkles.

**CUPCAKE TIP**
*For a cooked version
of this frosting, you can use
the recipe for Snow Frosting,
(page 42). You can also
use ready-made
marshmallow frosting if
you are in a hurry.*

# CHOCOLATE MALTED MILK SHAKE Cupcakes

These cupcakes remind me of those fabulous chocolate malted milk shakes we used to drink at the soda fountain of the local drug store when we were kids.

MAKES: **ABOUT 18 CUPCAKES**

¾ cup chocolate malted milk candies, crushed
½ cup chocolate malted milk powder
2 cups all-purpose flour
3 teaspoons baking powder
1 teaspoon salt
¾ cup/1½ sticks unsalted butter, room temperature
1 cup light brown sugar
2 eggs
1 teaspoon vanilla extract
1 cup half-and-half or light cream
CHOCOLATE MALTED MILK FROSTING
6 tablespoons/¾ stick unsalted butter, room temperature
⅓ cup chocolate malted milk powder
2 cups powdered sugar
Pinch of salt
¼ cup milk
1 teaspoon vanilla extract
Whipped cream (optional)
Chocolate malted milk candies

1. Preheat oven to 350°F.

2. In a small bowl, mix crushed chocolate malted milk candies, malted milk powder, flour, baking powder, and salt together. Set aside.

3. Cream butter and sugar until light and fluffy. Add eggs, one at a time, beating well after each addition. Add vanilla. Alternately add dry ingredients and half-and-half or light cream, beating until smooth after each addition.

4. Fill cupcake papers just a little over ½ full and bake for about 20 minutes or until a tester inserted into the center comes out clean. Remove from oven and cool.

5. To make the frosting: beat butter, malted milk powder, sugar, and salt until light and fluffy. Gradually add milk and vanilla, beating continuously, until frosting is of the desired consistency. You may want to use less milk. Frost cooled cupcakes, top with a dollop of whipped cream, if desired, and place a chocolate malted milk candy on top.

**CUPCAKE TIP**
*Replace cream with low-fat milk for a lighter version.*

# AFTER DINNER
## CUPCAKES

# BURGUNDY BLUES
## Cupcakes

Burgundy is one of the major wine-producing regions in France and some of the finest and best-known wines in the world are produced there. The combination of chocolate and red wine may seem strange at first but is actually quite delicious.

**MAKES: ABOUT 16–18 CUPCAKES**

¾ cup all-purpose flour
1 teaspoon baking powder
½ teaspoon salt
2 tablespoons instant cocoa powder (the presweetened kind)
1 teaspoon cinnamon
½ cup/1 stick unsalted butter, room temperature
½ cup sugar
2 eggs
¼ cup dry red wine
2 ounces grated dark chocolate

CHOCOLATE GLAZE
4 ounces good quality dark chocolate
¼ cup/½ stick unsalted butter
1 tablespoon corn syrup
Red and blue sugar for decoration

1. Preheat oven to 350°F.

2. Mix dry ingredients together and set aside.

3. Cream butter and sugar until light and fluffy. Add eggs, one at a time, mixing well after each addition. Alternately beat in flour mixture and wine. Fold in grated chocolate.

4. Spoon batter into cupcake papers, filling cups about ⅔ full. Bake for 20–25 minutes or until a tester inserted into the center comes out clean. Remove from oven and cool.

5. To make the chocolate glaze: melt chocolate and butter in a double boiler or a microwave. When just melted and barely warm to the touch, remove from heat and stir in corn syrup. Either dip cooled cupcakes in glaze or dribble a little over each cupcake. Sprinkle with red and blue sugar.

**CUPCAKE TIP**
*These cupcakes will go down particularly well with a glass of port wine or a cream sherry.*

# RUM RAISIN Cupcakes with Butter Rum Frosting

Rum and raisins are a very popular duo, and justifiably so. I think that the rum brings out the flavor of the raisins and vice versa. Make these in mini cupcake molds and serve them with rum and raisin ice cream for a special dessert treat.

**MAKES: ABOUT 16 REGULAR CUPCAKES OR 40 MINI-CUPCAKES**

½ cup raisins
¼ cup dark rum
1 cup, plus 2 tablespoons all-purpose flour
1½ teaspoons baking powder
1 teaspoon salt
½ cup/1 stick, plus 2 tablespoons unsalted butter, cut into small pieces
¾ cup light brown sugar
3 eggs, slightly beaten

BUTTER RUM FROSTING
¼ cup/½ stick unsalted butter, room temperature
2 cups powdered sugar
Pinch of salt
3 tablespoons rum (use raisin-soaking liquid)
Raisins for decoration

1. Soak raisins in rum for about 30 minutes, turning from time to time. Drain and set aside. Save liquid for frosting.

2. Preheat oven to 350°F.

3. In a large bowl, mix flour, baking powder, and salt together and set aside.

4. In a small pan, melt butter and sugar over low heat, stirring constantly. When sugar has dissolved, remove from heat and pour into the center of the flour mixture. Mix well. Add drained raisins and eggs and stir vigorously with a wooden spoon until the batter is smooth.

5. Fill cupcake papers about ⅔ full. Bake for about 25 minutes or until a tester inserted into the center comes out clean. Remove from oven and cool.

6. To make the frosting: cream butter, sugar, and salt until light and fluffy. Add rum and continue beating. If too thick, add more rum; if too thin, add more sugar. Frost cooled cupcakes and decorate with raisins.

# BEER & PEANUTS
## Cupcakes

These original and spectacular looking cupcakes will almost make you feel like you are sitting in a cosy pub in merry old England, downing a pint of ale and munching on some peanuts.

**MAKES: ABOUT 12–14 CUPCAKES**

1 cup dark beer
²/₃ cup light brown sugar
6 tablespoons/¾ stick unsalted butter, cut into pieces
½ cup raisins
1²/₃ cups all-purpose flour
2 teaspoons baking powder
1 teaspoon baking soda
1 teaspoon salt
1 teaspoon cinnamon
½ teaspoon ground ginger
Dash of grated nutmeg
2 eggs, slightly beaten

PEANUT BRITTLE TOPPING
6 tablespoons/¾ stick unsalted butter
1 cup light brown sugar
2 tablespoons sugar syrup (ready-made or boil equal amounts of sugar and water)
½ teaspoon lemon juice
1 cup grilled peanuts, lightly salted

1. In a large saucepan, bring beer, sugar, and butter to a boil. Add raisins and cook for 5 minutes over medium heat. Remove from heat and let cool, stirring from time to time so that a crust doesn't form.

2. Preheat oven to 350°F.

3. In a large bowl, mix dry ingredients together. Pour in cooled beer mixture and blend well. Add eggs, a little at a time, and continue mixing until batter is smooth.

4. Spoon batter into cupcake papers, filling cups about ½ full. Bake for about 15–20 minutes or until just starting to brown on top. Remember, they are going to cook for another 5–7 minutes.

5. While the cupcakes are cooking, make the topping. In a heavy pan, mix butter, sugar, syrup, and lemon juice and heat slowly until all of the sugar has dissolved, stirring from time to time. Continue to cook over low heat for another 5 minutes. Stir in peanuts and cook another 2 minutes.

6. Spread a layer of peanut topping over each cupcake. Return to oven and cook for 5–7 minutes. When peanuts start to brown, remove from oven and let cool in pan before removing cupcakes.

# KIR Cupcakes

The inspiration for these cupcakes is the "Kir," a cocktail made with white wine and black currant liqueur (Crème de Cassis). It originated in Dijon but is found in bars and on tables throughout France.

**MAKES: ABOUT 20 CUPCAKES**

1²/₃ cups all-purpose flour
1¹/₄ cups sugar
2 teaspoons baking powder
¹/₂ teaspoon salt, plus pinch for the
   egg whites
¹/₂ cup vegetable oil
¹/₂ cup white wine
4 eggs, separated
³/₄ cup dried currants

BLACK CURRANT GLAZE
6 ounces black currant jelly (about
   8 heaping tablespoons)
2 tablespoons black currant liqueur
   (optional)

FOR DECORATION
White decorator frosting
Red or black currants (optional)

1. Preheat oven to 350°F.

2. Mix flour, sugar, baking powder, and salt in a bowl. Gradually add liquid, mixing well. Add egg yolks, beating well after each addition. The batter should be smooth and light.

3. Beat egg whites with a pinch of salt until stiff but not dry. Gently fold into batter. Carefully fold in dried currants.

4. Fill cupcake papers about ³/₄ full with the mixture and bake for about 20 minutes or until a tester inserted into the center comes out clean. Remove from oven and cool.

5. To make the glaze: In a small pan, heat blackcurrant jelly with liqueur, if using, and cook for about 2 minutes. With a pastry brush, spread glaze on cooled cupcakes.

6. When glaze has cooled, decorate with a zigzag of white decorator frosting and fresh currants (red or black) if the season permits.

**CUPCAKE TIP**
*If you want to make a "Kir Royale," replace the white wine in the cupcake batter with champagne.*

# CAPPUCCINO
## Cupcakes

This light coffee cupcake with its meringue-like cooked coffee frosting is a delight to the eyes and a wonderful accompaniment to a real cappuccino at any time of the day.

**MAKES: ABOUT 12 CUPCAKES**

1 cup all-purpose flour
2 teaspoons baking powder
1 teaspoon salt
³/₄ cup/1¹/₂ sticks unsalted butter, room temperature
³/₄ cup brown sugar
2 eggs
1 tablespoon coffee extract
¹/₂ cup half-and-half or light cream

STEAMED COFFEE FROSTING
1¹/₄ cups brown sugar
3 tablespoons extra-strong coffee
2 egg whites
¹/₄ teaspoon baking powder or cream of tartar
Unsweetened cocoa powder or cinnamon for dusting
Chocolate sprinkles or chocolate coffee beans (optional) for decoration

1. Preheat oven to 350°F.

2. Sift flour, baking powder, and salt together and set aside.

3. Cream butter and sugar until light and fluffy. Add eggs, one at a time, blending well after each addition. Add coffee extract. Alternately add dry ingredients and half-and-half or cream, beating until smooth.

4. Divide batter between 12 cupcake papers. Cook for 25 minutes or until a tester inserted into the center comes out clean. Remove from oven and cool.

5. To make the frosting: mix all ingredients in the top of a double boiler. Place over rapidly boiling water and beat for about 7 minutes with an electric or rotary beater until frosting stands in peaks.

6. Remove from heat and spread on cupcakes or apply a generous spoonful to each cupcake. Sprinkle with cocoa powder before frosting hardens. Frosting will be hard on the outside and creamy on the inside. Sprinkle with chocolate sprinkles and put a chocolate coffee bean on top, if using. This is another variation on a 7-minute frosting.

# CUBA LIBRE
## Cupcakes

A "Cuba Libre" (Free Cuba) is generally a cocktail made with rum and cola and served with a lime wedge. Its origins are widely disputed but lets hope that its metamorphosis into a cupcake will meet with widespread approval!

**MAKES: ABOUT 12 CUPCAKES**

½ cup/1 stick unsalted butter, cut into small pieces
½ cup cola
1 cup all-purpose flour
1 teaspoon baking powder
1 teaspoon baking soda
½ teaspoon salt
1 cup sugar
¼ cup buttermilk
1 egg, slightly beaten
1 teaspoon vanilla extract

RUM FROSTING
½ cup/1 stick unsalted butter, room temperature
2 cups powdered sugar
Pinch of salt
2 tablespoons dark rum
Candied or jellied lime slices for decoration

1. In a medium saucepan, heat butter and cola until it boils. Remove from heat and let cool, about 10–15 minutes (you can set it in a pan of cold water to speed up the process).

2. Preheat oven to 350°F.

3. In a large mixing bowl, combine flour, baking powder, baking soda, salt, and sugar. Add cooled liquid to mixture and stir vigorously until batter is smooth and well blended. Beat in buttermilk, egg, and vanilla.

4. Spoon batter into cupcake papers, filling cups about ⅔ full. Bake for 20–25 minutes or until a tester inserted into the center comes out clean. Remove from oven and cool.

5. To make the frosting: cream butter, sugar, and salt until light and fluffy. Gradually add rum, beating continually until frosting is of spreading consistency. Frost cooled cupcakes. Decorate with candied or jellied lime slices.

# IRISH COFFEE
## Cupcakes

These cupcakes are a bit reminiscent of Irish soda bread, but with a dose of whiskey for good measure. The Mocha Butter Cream Frosting adds an elegant touch.

MAKES: **ABOUT 16 CUPCAKES**

1½ cups all-purpose flour
¾ cup brown sugar
1 teaspoon baking powder
1 teaspoon baking soda
1 teaspoon salt
1 teaspoon cinnamon
½ teaspoon ground ginger
Dash of grated nutmeg
½ cup dark raisins
½ cup coarsely chopped nuts
   (pistachios, walnuts, or hazelnuts)
2 eggs, slightly beaten
½ cup vegetable oil
½ cup Irish whiskey
¼ cup light cream or milk

MOCHA BUTTER CREAM FROSTING
1 cup/2 sticks unsalted butter, room
   temperature, cut into small pieces
1⅔ cups powdered sugar
2 egg yolks
1 tablespoon coffee extract or very
   strong coffee (more or less,
   depending on your taste)

1. Preheat oven to 350°F.

2. In a large bowl, mix all of the dry ingredients together. Add eggs, oil, whiskey, and cream or milk to dry ingredients and mix until thoroughly blended with a wooden spoon.

3. Fill cupcake papers about ⅔ full. Bake for 25–30 minutes or until a tester inserted into the center comes out clean. Remove from oven and cool.

4. To make the frosting: cream butter and sugar together until light and fluffy. Add egg yolks and coffee extract to taste and beat until mixture is light, shiny, and of good spreading consistency (at least 10 minutes). Frost cooled cupcakes.

**CUPCAKE TIP**
*If you don't have the time or are otherwise inclined, frost these cupcakes with coffee-flavored whipped cream or use the Irish Whiskey Frosting (page 124).*

# MINT JULEP
## Cupcakes

A mint julep is a cocktail composed of fresh mint, bourbon, and crushed ice. It is traditionally served in an iced pewter or silver mug during the Kentucky Derby.

**MAKES: ABOUT 18 CUPCAKES**

1 cup all-purpose flour
1 teaspoon baking powder
1 teaspoon salt
¾ cup/1½ sticks unsalted butter, room temperature
1 cup sugar
3 eggs
½ cup bourbon
¼ cup fresh finely chopped mint

WHITE CHOCOLATE MINT FROSTING
½ cup whipping cream
1 tablespoon unsalted butter
8 ounces white chocolate
2 tablespoons crème de menthe (or any other mint liqueur)
Green food coloring (optional)
Several sprigs of fresh mint for decoration
Green sugar (optional) for decoration
Decorative straws

1. Preheat oven to 350°F.

2. Mix flour, baking powder, and salt together and set aside.

3. Cream butter and sugar until light and fluffy. Add eggs, one at a time, mixing well after each addition. Alternately beat in flour mixture and bourbon. Fold in fresh mint.

4. Spoon batter into cupcake papers, filling cups about ⅔ full. Bake for 20–25 minutes or until a tester inserted into the center comes out clean. Remove from oven and cool.

5. To make the frosting: heat cream and butter in a pan over medium heat, stirring until butter melts. Remove from heat and add white chocolate. Stir until melted. Add mint liqueur and food coloring, if desired. Transfer frosting to a bowl and let cool, stirring from time to time, until it is of spreading consistency. This will probably take about 2 hours. You can speed up the process by putting the bowl in cold water.

6. Frost cooled cupcakes and decorate with a sprig of mint. Alternatively, you can dip the cupcakes in the frosting once the mixture has cooled a bit. Decorate immediately with green sugar and a mint sprig before frosting hardens. Stick in a little straw for good measure.

# MEZZO-MEZZO Cupcakes

Chocolate and coffee are an irresistible duo. These sour cream cupcakes will be a gourmet ending to any gourmet meal.

MAKES: ABOUT 16 REGULAR CUPCAKES, 8 JUMBO CUPCAKES, OR 40 MINI-CUPCAKES

1⅓ cups all-purpose flour
2 teaspoons baking powder
1 teaspoon baking soda
1 teaspoon salt
½ cup unsweetened cocoa powder
1 cup light brown sugar
3 tablespoons instant cappuccino powder (you can use espresso or even decaffeinated coffee powder)
½ cup/1 stick unsalted butter, melted and cooled
2 eggs, slightly beaten
1 cup sour cream

CHOCOLATE WHIPPED CREAM FROSTING
1 cup heavy whipping cream, chilled
3 tablespoons sugar
1 tablespoon unsweetened cocoa powder, plus more for dusting
1 tablespoon instant cappuccino powder (you can use espresso or decaffeinated coffee powder)
Chocolate coffee beans for decoration

1. Preheat oven to 350°F.

2. In a large bowl, mix all of the dry ingredients together and set aside.

3. In another bowl, mix butter, eggs, and sour cream together. Pour into dry ingredients, rapidly mixing with a wooden spoon until batter is smooth.

4. Spoon batter into cupcake papers, filling cups about ⅔ full. Cook for 15–20 minutes or until a tester inserted into the center comes out clean. Remove from oven and cool.

5. To make the frosting: put cream, sugar, cocoa, and coffee powder in a large bowl. Stir, cover, and let sit in the refrigerator for about an hour, until chocolate and coffee have dissolved. Remove from refrigerator and beat with an electric beater until stiff.

6. Frost cooled cupcakes just before serving. Dust with cocoa powder and top each cupcake with a chocolate coffee bean.

**CUPCAKE TIP**
*Serve with
a little cup of
espresso
on the side.*

# MARGARITA
## Cupcakes with Lime Glaze

For this cupcake version of a margarita cocktail, I have recommended using coarse sugar to imitate the salt but if you are particularly daring you could put a few grains of "fleur de sel" on top. The contrast of the very sweet lime glaze and the salt would certainly take one back to this cupcake's origins.

**MAKES: ABOUT 18 CUPCAKES**

1 cup all-purpose flour
1 teaspoon baking powder
½ teaspoon salt, plus pinch for the egg whites
½ cup/1 stick unsalted butter, room temperature
¾ cup sugar
3 eggs, separated
1 tablespoon finely grated lime rind
2 tablespoons tequila

LIME GLAZE
2 tablespoons fresh lime juice
1 cup powdered sugar
1 tablespoon tequila
Green food coloring (optional)
Coarse sugar (or salt, see step 6)
Jellied lime slices for decoration

1. Preheat oven to 350°F.

2. Mix flour, baking powder, and salt together and set aside.

3. Cream butter and sugar until light and fluffy. Add egg yolks, one at a time, mixing well after each addition. Add lime rind and tequila. Gradually stir in dry ingredients until all of the flour is absorbed and the batter is smooth.

4. Beat egg whites with a pinch of salt until stiff but not dry. Gently fold whites into batter.

5. Fill cupcake papers a little over ½ full. Bake for about 20–25 minutes or until a tester inserted into the center comes out clean. Remove from oven and cool.

6. To make the glaze: in a medium bowl, mix the lime juice, powdered sugar, and tequila and beat until smooth and blended. Stir in green food coloring, if desired. Brush cooled cupcakes with glaze and sprinkle with coarse sugar (or a few grains of "fleur de sel"). Decorate with a jellied lime slice.

# MIDNIGHT MADNESS
## Cupcakes

Wait until midnight and surprise your guests
with these indulgent little black gems.

**MAKES: ABOUT 20 CUPCAKES**

1¼ cups all-purpose flour
¾ cup light brown sugar
¼ cup unsweetened cocoa powder
2 teaspoons baking powder
½ teaspoon salt
¾ cup water
¼ cup vegetable oil
1 egg, lightly beaten
1 teaspoon vanilla extract

FILLING
1 cup/8 ounces cream cheese
⅓ cup sugar
1 egg
½ teaspoon salt
1 tablespoon rum or brandy (optional)
3 ounces chocolate chips

MIDNIGHT SKY FROSTING
2½ cups powdered sugar
2 egg whites
Pinch of salt or cream of tartar
Black food coloring

FOR DECORATION
Glitter sugar for dusting
Silver balls and candy banana shape

1. Preheat oven to 350°F.

2. To make the filling: beat cream cheese, sugar, egg, salt, and rum until smooth. Fold in chocolate chips and set aside.

3. Mix flour, sugar, cocoa powder, baking powder, and salt in a large bowl. Add water, oil, egg, and vanilla and beat with a wooden spoon until smooth.

4. Fill cupcake papers ½ full with chocolate batter. Place a heaping teaspoon of the cream cheese mixture on each. Bake for about 15–25 minutes or until firm to the touch. The cream cheese filling will be a bit soft. Remove from oven and cool.

5. To make the frosting: using an electric beater, beat sugar with egg whites and salt or cream of tartar until mixed. Increase speed to high and beat for about 5 minutes or until very thick and fluffy. Add black food coloring. Frost cooled cupcakes and dust with glitter sugar, silver balls and candy banana shape for the moon.

**CUPCAKE TIP**
*Alternatively, instead of making Midnight Sky Frosting you could top with ready-to-use black cake frosting.*

# PINA COLADA
## Cupcakes

The main ingredients in a Piña Colada cocktail, just like in this cupcake, are pineapple, coconut, and rum. Sit back, enjoy, and listen to the palm trees swaying in the ocean breeze.

**MAKES: ABOUT 16–18 CUPCAKES**

2 cups all-purpose flour
2 teaspoons baking powder
1 teaspoon salt, plus pinch for the
    egg whites
½ cup/1 stick unsalted butter, room
    temperature
1¼ cups sugar
2 eggs, separated
½ cup pineapple juice
¼ cup light rum (or coconut cream or
    more pineapple juice)
½ cup shredded coconut

COCONUT ICING

2 egg whites
Pinch of salt
2 cups powdered sugar
½ cup shredded coconut

FOR DECORATION

Toasted shredded coconut
Dried or crystallized pineapple

1. Preheat oven to 350°F.

2. Mix together flour, baking powder, and salt together in a bowl and set aside.

3. Cream butter and sugar until light and fluffy. Add egg yolks, one at a time, mixing well after each addition. Alternately beat in flour mixture and liquid and blend until smooth. Stir in coconut. Beat egg whites with pinch of salt until stiff but not dry and gently fold into mixture.

4. Spoon batter into cupcake papers, filling cups about ⅔ full, smoothing with the back of a spoon. Bake for 20–25 minutes or until a tester inserted into the center comes out clean. Remove from oven and cool.

5. To make the icing: beat egg whites with a pinch of salt until stiff but not dry. Add sugar by heaping tablespoons, beating continually. Fold in shredded coconut. Add additional powdered sugar if necessary so that icing holds its shape. Ice cooled cupcakes and sprinkle with toasted coconut and a piece of dried or crystallized pineapple.

# PASTIS Cupcakes with Anise Frosting

"Pastis" is an anise-based liqueur, diluted with water, and extremely popular in the south of France as an aperitif. Any brand will do. The result is surprising and extraordinary—a delicate anise-flavored batter, topped with creamy anise-flavored butter cream frosting.

**MAKES: ABOUT 18 CUPCAKES**

1½ cups all-purpose flour
2 teaspoons baking powder
1 teaspoon salt
¾ cups/1½ sticks unsalted butter, room temperature
¾ cup sugar
3 eggs
¼ cup pastis

ANISE BUTTER CREAM FROSTING
1 cup/2 sticks unsalted butter, room temperature, cut into small pieces
1⅔ cups powdered sugar
Pinch of salt
2 tablespoons pastis (or anise syrup or licorice essence to taste)
Liqcorice strands, licorice candies, or black decorator frosting for decoration

1. Preheat oven to 350°F.

2. Mix flour, baking powder, and salt together and set aside.

3. Cream butter and sugar until light and fluffy. Add eggs, one at a time, mixing well after each addition. Alternately beat in flour mixture and pastis.

4. Spoon batter into cupcake papers, filling cups about ⅔ full. Bake for 25 minutes or until a tester inserted into the center comes out clean. Remove from oven and cool.

5. To make the frosting: in the large bowl of an electric mixer, beat butter, sugar, and salt until light and fluffy. Add pastis and continue beating until of good spreading consistency. Frost cooled cupcakes. Decorate with a strand of licorice (arranged in a spiral shape over the icing), licorice candies, or black decorator frosting.

**CUPCAKE TIP**
*If you prefer, use anise syrup for a non-alcoholic version.*

# AFTER EIGHT Cupcakes

These cupcakes will dazzle the eyes as well as the taste buds. When you bite into them—crispy on the outside and creamy on the inside—chocolate mint heaven, beyond a doubt!

**MAKES: ABOUT 12 CUPCAKES**

1⅓ cups all-purpose flour
⅓ cup unsweetened cocoa powder
2 teaspoons baking powder
1 teaspoon salt
6 tablespoons/¾ stick unsalted butter, room temperature
½ cup sugar
2 eggs
⅔ cup half-and-half or light cream
Few drops of mint extract
½ cup miniature chocolate mint chips

MINT BUTTER CREAM FROSTING
¾ cup/1½ sticks unsalted butter, room temperature, cut into small pieces
2 cups powdered sugar
2 tablespoons milk
Few drops of mint extract
Food coloring (optional)

CHOCOLATE GANACHE
5 ounces dark chocolate, broken into little pieces
⅔ cup heavy cream
12 little chocolate-covered mint patties (optional) for decoration

1. Preheat oven to 350°F.

2. Mix flour, cocoa, baking powder, and salt together and set aside.

3. Cream butter and sugar until light and fluffy. Add eggs, one at a time, mixing after each addition. Alternately beat in flour mixture and half-and-half or cream. Add a few drops of mint extract to batter and mix well.

4. Spoon batter into 12 cupcake papers. Sprinkle chocolate mint chips over cupcakes and bake for 20–25 minutes or until a tester inserted into the center comes out clean. Remove from oven and cool.

5. To make the frosting: cream butter and sugar until light and fluffy. Add milk and mint extract and mix well. You may want to add more or less milk. Add food coloring if you are using it. Spread over cooled cupcakes and set in a cool place until frosting has hardened.

6. To make the ganache: place chocolate and cream in a double boiler or a microwave and heat until cream is warm to the touch and the chocolate starts to melt. Remove from heat and stir until all of the chocolate has melted and the mixture is homogeneous. Remember—you don't want to cook the chocolate, you just want to melt it. You can always put it back over the warm water or in the microwave for a few seconds if you need to. Cool slightly and dip cupcakes in chocolate ganache, leaving a little of the butter cream showing around the edges. Place a little chocolate-covered mint patty on top, if desired.

# GOURMET
# CUPCAKES

# TARTE TATIN Cupcakes with Caramelized Apples

A Tarte Tatin is a French upside-down apple tart, one of the simplest and most delicious of traditional French desserts and very popular in my family, especially in the fall when the apples are at their finest. This is my cupcake version.

**MAKES: ABOUT 16 CUPCAKES**

1²/₃ cups all-purpose flour
2 teaspoons baking powder
1 teaspoon salt
1 cup packed brown sugar
¹/₂ cup/1 stick unsalted butter, room temperature
2 eggs, slightly beaten
¹/₂ cup milk
1 teaspoon vanilla extract

CARAMELIZED APPLES
¹/₄ cup/¹/₂ stick unsalted butter
4 apples, peeled, cored, and cut into 16 (cut each quarter into four parts, lengthwise)
4 tablespoons sugar

CARAMEL GLAZE
¹/₄ cup/¹/₂ stick butter
¹/₄ cup firmly packed brown sugar
1¹/₂ cups powdered sugar
1 teaspoon vanilla extract
1 tablespoon milk

**1.** Preheat oven to 350°F.

**2.** In a large bowl, mix flour, baking powder, salt, and sugar. Add remaining cupcake ingredients and beat with a wooden spoon or whisk for 3 minutes.

**3.** Spoon batter into cupcake papers, filling about ²/₃ full. Bake for about 20 minutes or until a tester inserted into the center comes out clean. Remove from oven and cool.

**4.** To caramelize the apples: in a large pan, melt the butter and lay out the pieces of apple, cooking them on both sides. When they are golden, sprinkle them with sugar and remove from heat. Arrange them attractively on the cupcakes, four apple sections per cupcake. You may want to cook the apples in two batches.

**5.** To make the glaze (or use ready-made caramel if you prefer): melt butter in a heavy pan over low heat. Add brown sugar and stir for about 3 minutes until sugar is melted. Remove from heat. Add powdered sugar, vanilla, and milk and blend with a whisk. Dribble about a tablespoon of caramel over each cupcake.

# BOURDALOUE Cupcakes with Caramelized Almonds

Any preparation with the adjective "Bourdaloue" attached to it means that it is prepared with some combination of pears and almonds. A cupcake "à la Bourdaloue"—you guessed it—has pears and almonds as its main ingredients! These cupcakes are made in jumbo cupcake molds and are not only delicious but are impressive to behold.

**MAKES: ABOUT 6–8 JUMBO CUPCAKES**

¾ cup/1½ sticks unsalted butter, room temperature
½ cup sugar
3 eggs
2 teaspoons vanilla extract
1½ cups ground almonds
¼ cup all-purpose flour
1 teaspoon salt
6–8 pear halves, (fresh or canned), cut lengthwise into quarters

CARAMELIZED ALMONDS
1 cup slivered almonds
¼ cup sugar

**1.** Preheat oven to 350°F.

**2.** Cream butter and sugar together until light and fluffy. Add eggs, one at a time, blending well after each addition. Add vanilla. Add ground almonds, flour, and salt and mix until batter is smooth.

**3.** Divide batter between 6–8 jumbo cupcake papers. Place a pear quarters in the center, pressing in just slightly. Cook for 30 minutes or until cupcakes are golden brown and spring back to the touch. Remove from oven and cool before unmolding.

**4.** Mix almonds and sugar in a cold nonstick pan. Turn heat to high, stirring constantly. When almonds start to brown (this will take only a few minutes), pour them immediately into a heat-proof dish. When they are completely cool, gently break them loose with a fork or your fingers. Sprinkle them over cupcakes just before serving.

**CUPCAKE TIP**
*Bake these in a silicon mold and serve with custard sauce ( see page 164)*

# CEVENOL Cupcakes with Crème de Marron icing

The Cevennes mountains in the south of France are known for their rustic landscapes and the chestnut trees that grow on their gentle slopes. Robert Louis Stevenson immortalized the Cevennes in a book that he wrote about a trip he took through these mountains with a donkey. The area is also known for its many local specialties made from chestnuts.

**MAKES: ABOUT 16 CUPCAKES**

²/₃ cup all-purpose flour

2 teaspoons baking powder

1 teaspoon salt

5 tablespoons unsalted butter

2 cups "crème de marron" chestnut spread (can be found in most gourmet food stores)

¹/₂ cup sugar

2 eggs

2 tablespoons rum

8 glazed chestnuts (can be found in most gourmet food stores) for decoration

1. Preheat oven to 350°F.

2. Mix flour, baking powder, and salt together and set aside.

3. In the large bowl of an electric mixer, cream butter and 1 cup chestnut spread until smooth and creamy. Add sugar, eggs, and rum and beat until thoroughly blended. Mix in dry ingredients.

4. Spoon batter into cupcake papers, filling about ²/₃ full. Bake for about 25 minutes or until a tester inserted into the center comes out clean. Remove from oven and cool.

5. Ice cooled cupcakes with remaining chestnut spread and top each cupcake with half a glazed chestnut.

# CRÈPE SUZETTE Cupcakes

A "Crèpe Suzette" is a crepe that is filled with a butter cream made with orange liqueur (Grand Marnier, Cointreau, Triple Sec, Curaçao, etc.) and flambéed before being eaten. This is the cupcake version, frosted with the same cream I use for my Crèpes Suzettes.

**MAKES: ABOUT 12 CUPCAKES**

2 cups all-purpose flour
2 teaspoons baking powder
1 teaspoon salt
½ cup/1 stick unsalted butter, room temperature
¾ cup sugar
2 eggs
Juice and finely grated rind of 1 medium-sized orange
2 tablespoons orange liqueur (Grand Marnier, Cointreau, Triple Sec, Curaçao, etc.)
Water, if necessary

SUZETTE FROSTING
⅔ cup/1¼ sticks unsalted butter, room temperature
¾ cup sugar
Juice and finely grated rind of 1 medium orange or two small tangerines
¼ cup orange liqueur
Candied orange peel for decoration

1. Preheat oven to 350°F.

2. Mix flour, baking powder, and salt together. Set aside.

3. Cream butter and sugar until light and fluffy. Add eggs, one at a time, beating thoroughly after each addition. Add orange rind. Combine orange juice and orange liqueur and add water, if necessary, to make ½ cup. Alternately add dry ingredients and liquid to butter mixture, blending until batter is smooth.

4. Fill cupcake papers about ⅔ full and bake for about 20–25 minutes or until a tester inserted into the center comes out clean. Remove from oven and cool.

5. To make the frosting: cream butter with sugar until it is light and fluffy. Slowly add the juice and rind of the orange or tangerines, beating continually. Carefully add the liqueur, little by little, making sure that the mixture doesn't curdle. Keep beating until mixture is of spreading consistency. Frost cooled cupcakes and decorate with a piece of candied orange peel. The butter will harden when it sets so make sure to frost the cupcakes while the frosting is still creamy.

**CUPCAKE TIP**
*Suzette frosting is a challenge. You can replace it with any other orange frosting (see page 137)*

# CHOCOLATE MOUSSE Cupcakes

The chocolate mousse cake that inspired this recipe was and still is my son's preferred birthday cake recipe. This 2-in-1 recipe includes both the batter and the frosting for these light and very moist cupcakes. For chocoholics only!

**MAKES: ABOUT 12 CUPCAKES**

4 heaping tablespoons all-purpose flour
2½ teaspoons baking powder
½ teaspoon salt, plus good pinch for the egg whites
10 ounces dark chocolate
1 cup/2 sticks unsalted butter, room temperature
6 eggs, separated
1 cup sugar
Grated chocolate for decoration

**CUPCAKE TIP**
*You might want to double this recipe—you will never have too many.*

1. Preheat oven to 350°F.

2. Mix flour, baking powder, and salt together and set aside.

3. Melt the chocolate and butter in a double boiler or microwave. Don't cook—the chocolate and butter should be just melted. Stir and set aside.

4. Beat egg yolks and sugar until light yellow and foamy. Beat in the melted chocolate until totally blended.

5. Beat egg whites with a pinch of salt until stiff but not dry. Gently fold into chocolate mixture. Divide mixture into two parts and put one of them in the refrigerator to be used later to frost cupcakes. Gently whisk flour mixture into other half until it is completely absorbed.

6. Fill cupcake papers about ⅔ full with batter and bake for 15–20 minutes. Don't overcook. Cupcakes should be just cooked and moist in the center. Remove from oven and cool.

7. When cupcakes are cool, frost with remaining chocolate mousse. Decorate with grated chocolate.

# EARL GREY Cupcakes

The distinctive taste of Earl Grey tea is due to bergamot, a small tree in the orange family. The rind of the bergamot orange yields an aromatic oil, used in the tea and perfume industries.

**MAKES: 12 CUPCAKES**

⅔ cup whole milk
2 teaspoons loose or 2 tea bags
  Earl Grey tea
1½ cups all-purpose flour
2 teaspoons baking powder
1 teaspoons salt
½ cup/1 stick unsalted butter, room
  temperature
1 cup sugar
2 eggs
3 tablespoons candied orange rind,
  chopped into little pieces
  (optional)

CHOCOLATE EARL GREY GANACHE
6 ounces good quality dark chocolate,
  broken into pieces
1 tablespoon unsalted butter, room
  temperature
½ cup heavy cream
2 teaspoons loose or 2 tea bags
  Earl Grey tea

1. In a small pan, heat milk with tea. Bring to a boil and then remove from heat and let steep until milk is cool to the touch, about 30 minutes. Filter the tea or remove tea bags and set liquid aside.

2. Preheat oven to 350°F.

3. Mix flour, baking powder, and salt together and set aside.

4. Cream butter and sugar together until light and fluffy. Add eggs, one at a time, mixing well after each addition. Alternately beat in dry ingredients and liquid. Fold in candied orange rind, if desired.

5. Spoon batter into cupcake papers, filling cups about ⅔ full. Bake for about 25 minutes or until a tester inserted into the center comes out clean. Remove from oven and cool.

6. To make the ganache: put chocolate and butter in a large mixing bowl and set aside.  Combine cream and tea in a small pan and slowly bring to a boil. Remove from heat, cover, and let tea steep in cream for at least 30 minutes.

7. Boil mixture once again and strain over the bowl with chocolate and butter. Let sit for about 2 minutes until chocolate and butter have started to melt and then whisk until smooth. Put ganache in the refrigerator until it is thick enough (but not too thick!) to spread over cupcakes. You can also wait until it cools and beat it with an electric beater for about 5–10 minutes for a lighter, creamier chocolate frosting.

# CRÈME BRULÉE Cupcakes

Crème Brulée literally means "burnt cream." Basically, it is a vanilla custard that is chilled, sprinkled with sugar just before serving, and placed under a broiler so that the sugar burns and forms a crust. There are many variations on the theme. Here is a cupcake one.

**MAKES: ABOUT 16 CUPCAKES**

2½ cups all-purpose flour
3 teaspoons baking powder
½ teaspoon salt, plus pinch for the egg whites
½ cup/1 stick unsalted butter, room temperature
1½ cups sugar
2 eggs, separated
1 cup milk
3 tablespoons caramel syrup (the kind used for ice cream sundaes)
1 teaspoon vanilla extract

BROWN SUGAR FROSTING
1½ cups dark brown sugar
¾ cup granulated sugar
Pinch of salt
½ cup milk
3 tablespoons unsalted butter, cut into pieces
2 tablespoons corn syrup
2 teaspoons vanilla extract
Brown sugar for sprinkling

1. Preheat oven to 350°F.

2. Mix flour, baking powder, and salt together and set aside.

3. Cream butter and sugar together until light and fluffy. Add egg yolks, one at a time, mixing well after each addition. Alternately beat in dry ingredients and milk. Add caramel syrup and vanilla. Beat until smooth.

4. Beat egg whites with a pinch of salt until stiff but not dry. Gently fold whites into batter.

5. Spoon batter into cupcake papers, filling cups about ⅔ full. Bake for about 20 minutes or until a tester inserted into the center comes out clean. Remove from oven and cool.

6. Mix all the frosting ingredients except the vanilla in a heavy pan over low heat. Slowly bring mixture to a boil, stirring constantly, and boil for 1 minute. Remove from heat and cool until just warm to the touch. Add vanilla and beat until thick enough to spread. Frost cooled cupcakes and sprinkle with brown sugar.

**CUPCAKE TIP**
*You can substitute the vanilla in the cupcake batter with lavender extract, orange flower water, or rose water to add your own individual touch.*

# THE ARLÉSIENNE

When I had my restaurant in the south of France, one of my most popular summer desserts was a tart made with fresh apricots, almonds, and raspberry jelly, known as the "Arlésienne." Arles is a lovely little city, located in Provence, on the banks of the Rhone river and in the middle of the Camargue, home to wild horses and pink flamingos. Provence abounds with apricot trees, almond trees, whose lovely pink blossoms announce the arrival of spring, and raspberries. The combination is definitely a winner.

**MAKES: ABOUT 12 CUPCAKES**

1½ cups all-purpose flour
2 teaspoons baking powder
1 teaspoon salt
½ cup/1 stick unsalted butter, room
    temperature
½ cup sugar
2 eggs
5 tablespoons milk
Few drops of almond extract
    (optional)
½ cup dried apricots, or dried
    raspberries (or a combination of
    both), cut into little cubes
½ cup coarsely ground almonds
6 small apricots, halved
12 teaspoons raspberry jelly

1. Preheat oven to 350°F.

2. Mix flour, baking powder, and salt together and set aside.

3. Cream butter and sugar until light and fluffy. Add eggs, one at a time, mixing well after each addition. Alternately beat in flour mixture and milk. Add almond extract to taste. Fold in dried apricots and almonds.

4. Spoon batter into cupcake papers, filling a little over ½ full. Place an apricot half in the top of each cupcake, hollow side up, pressing gently into batter. Put a teaspoon of raspberry jelly in each hollow. Bake for 20–25 minutes or until a tester inserted into the center comes out clean and the tops are golden brown. Remove from oven and cool.

**CUPCAKE TIP**
*The picture opposite depicts the cupcakes before they are baked. They should be a lovely golden color when cooked.*

# PECHE MELBA Cupcakes

Try this very easy one-bowl cupcake version of the popular dessert. If you prefer you could bake the cupcakes in silicon molds and serve with Raspberry Sauce and whipped cream.

**MAKES: ABOUT 16 CUPCAKES**

3 eggs, slightly beaten
1½ cups sugar
½ cup vegetable oil
2 cups all-purpose flour
2 teaspoons baking powder
1 teaspoon salt
1 teaspoon cinnamon (optional)
2 cups fresh, canned, or frozen
   peaches, cut into pieces (set aside
   enough thin slices to decorate
   cupcakes)

RASPBERRY CREAM FROSTING
1 cup heavy whipping cream, chilled
3 tablespoons sugar
½ cup slightly sweetened raspberry
   purée (if you are using fresh
   raspberries, purée them with a
   fork or in a food processor with
   1 tablespoon sugar)

RASPBERRY SAUCE
2 cups raspberries (set a few aside
   to decorate cupcakes)
½ cup sugar
¼ cup water
Few drops lemon juice
Whipped cream for decoration

1. Preheat oven to 350°F.

2. In a large bowl, mix all of the cupcake ingredients apart from the peaches with a wooden spoon. Gently fold in peaches.

3. Spoon batter into cupcake papers, filling about ⅔ full. Bake for about 25 minutes or until a tester inserted into the center comes out clean. Remove from oven and cool.

4. Make either Raspberry Whipped Cream Frosting or Raspberry Sauce. For frosting: beat cream with sugar until soft peaks form. Gradually add raspberry purée, beating continually. Beat until stiff peaks form. Add more sugar, if necessary. Frost cupcakes just before serving and decorate with a peach slice.

5. To make the sauce: wash and clean raspberries. Slowly heat raspberries and sugar in a medium pan with water. When mixture starts to boil, cook for 1 minute and remove from heat. Purée by hand or in a food processor with a few drops lemon juice. Spoon raspberry sauce over cupcakes. Serve with a dollop of whipped cream and a fresh raspberry.

**CUPCAKE TIP**
*The Raspberry Sauce
can be kept in the
refrigerator or frozen
for later use.*

# THE LANGUEDOCIENNE

Languedoc is a region in southern France known for its abundant sunshine, fields of lavender, figs, goat cheese, honey, and great wines. These cupcakes embody the spirit of the region. Enjoy them after a meal with a glass of sweet Muscat wine.

**MAKES: ABOUT 16 CUPCAKES**

¾ cup honey
½ cup brown sugar
¼ cup/½ stick unsalted butter, cut into pieces
3 tablespoons milk
1⅔ cups all-purpose flour
2 teaspoons baking powder
1 teaspoon salt
1 tablespoon dried lavender (optional)
2 eggs
1 cup dried figs, cut into little pieces (save a few pieces for the decoration)

GOAT CHEESE FROSTING
¾ cup very fresh goat cheese or creamy goat's cheese such as Chavroux (can be found in most supermarkets)
2 tablespoons/¼ stick unsalted butter, softened
1½ cups powdered sugar

1. In a medium pan, heat honey, sugar, butter, and milk over very low heat. Stir until the sugar has dissolved and remove from heat. Let cool.

2. Preheat oven to 350°F.

3. Mix flour, baking powder, salt, and lavender together. Add to cooled honey mixture and beat well with a wooden spoon. Add eggs, one by one, beating well after each addition. Fold figs into batter.

4. Fill cupcake papers about ⅔ full. Bake for about 25 minutes or until a tester inserted into the center comes out clean.

5. To make the frosting: cream goat cheese, butter, and sugar until smooth and well blended. If frosting is too soft or liquid, place it in the refrigerator until it is of good spreading consistency. Put a dollop of frosting on each cupcake and decorate with a piece of dried fig.

**CUPCAKE TIP**
*If you can't get goat cheese, use cream cheese instead.*

# RICOTTA LIME
## Cupcakes with Lime Glaze

These light and airy cupcakes will be as welcome as a lime cooler on a hot summer's day. You can dust them with powdered sugar or use a lime glaze that will look very cool with a dollop of whipped cream, sprinkled with green sugar, and topped with a candied or jellied lime section.

**MAKES: ABOUT 16 CUPCAKES**

1¼ cups all-purpose flour
1½ teaspoons baking powder
1 teaspoon salt, plus pinch for the egg whites
Juice (about 3 tablespoons) and finely grated rind of 1 lime
5 tablespoons unsalted butter, room temperature
¾ cup sugar
⅓ cup ricotta cheese
3 eggs, separated
LIME GLAZE
2 tablespoons freshly squeezed lime juice
½ cup powdered sugar
FOR DECORATION
Whipped cream (optional)
Green sugar
Candied or jellied lime sections

1. Preheat oven to 350°F.

2. Mix flour, baking powder, salt, and lime rind together and set aside.

3. Cream butter and sugar together until light and fluffy. Add ricotta, beating until smooth. Add egg yolks, one at a time, blending well after each addition. Add flour mixture and lime juice and mix well.

4. Beat egg whites with a pinch of salt until stiff but not dry. Gently fold whites into batter.

5. Spoon batter into cupcake papers, filling cups about ⅔ full. Bake for about 20–25 minutes or until a tester inserted into the center comes out clean. Remove from oven and cool.

6. To make the frosting: in a small bowl, combine lime juice and sugar and whisk until smooth. Spread over cooled cupcakes with a pastry brush. Decorate whipped cream with green sugar and a candied or jellied lime section.

# TIRAMISU Cupcakes with Mascarpone Cream

Tiramisu is an Italian cake usually made with sponge cake or ladyfingers soaked in a mixture of coffee and Marsala, filled with mascarpone cream and topped with grated chocolate. Here is one cupcake version.

**MAKES: ABOUT 12 CUPCAKES**

1 cup all-purpose flour
1 teaspoon baking powder
½ teaspoon salt
2 eggs, separated
¼ cup very strong coffee
1 tablespoon Marsala or 1 tablespoon Kahlua or 1 teaspoon vanilla extract
¾ cup sugar
Pinch of salt
Extra Marsala for sprinkling (optional)

**MASCARPONE CREAM**
2 egg yolks
3 teaspoons sugar
1 tablespoon Kahlua (optional)
1 cup mascarpone
Kahlua for drizzling
Grated chocolate for decoration

1. Preheat oven to 350°F.

2. Mix flour, baking powder, and salt together and set aside.

3. Beat egg yolks with coffee and Marsala until very thick and creamy. Gradually add ½ cup of the sugar, beating continually. Set aside.

4. Beat egg whites with salt until they start to form moist peaks and gradually beat in remaining ¼ cup sugar. Continue beating until egg whites are stiff but not dry. Stir 3 tablespoons of the whites into yolk mixture. Gradually fold dry ingredients into mixture, using a whisk. When the dry ingredients have been absorbed, gently fold in remaining whites.

5. Spoon batter into 12 cupcake papers, filling about ⅔ full. Bake for about 20 minutes or until a tester inserted into the center comes out clean. Remove from oven and cool.

6. When cupcakes are cool, you can poke tops with a fork a few times and sprinkle a tablespoon of Marsala over each cupcake, if desired.

7. To make the mascarpone cream: beat egg yolks with sugar until they are light and fluffy. Beat in Kahlua, if desired. Gradually add mascarpone, beating continually. Pile cream on cupcakes, drizzle with kahlua, and sprinkle with chocolate.

# LINZERTORTE
## Cupcakes

These cupcakes are an adaptation of a recipe from my friend Hannelore, who grew up on her Austrian mother's linzertortes, to which she added a touch of chocolate to give them more body.

**MAKES: ABOUT 12 CUPCAKES**

¾ cups/1½ sticks unsalted butter, room temperature
1 cup all-purpose flour
½ teaspoon salt, plus good pinch for the egg whites
3 tablespoons unsweetened cocoa powder
1½ cups powdered sugar
¾ cup ground almonds
¾ cup ground hazelnuts
6 egg whites
Good pinch of salt
Raspberry jelly, (see method)
Whipped cream or decorator frosting
Hazelnuts or almonds, halved, for decoration
Powdered sugar for dusting

**1.** Preheat oven to 350°F.

**2.** In a small pan, melt butter, letting it brown just slightly. Remove from heat and cool.

**3.** In a large bowl, mix flour, salt, cocoa powder, powdered sugar, ground almonds, and hazelnuts together. Set aside.

**4.** Beat egg whites with a pinch of salt until they are foamy but not stiff.

**5.** Make a well in the middle of the dry ingredients and add egg whites and cooled butter. Mix well.

**6.** Spoon batter into cupcake papers, filling about ⅔ full. Bake for about 20–25 minutes or until a tester inserted into the center comes out clean. Remove from oven and cool.

**7.** When cupcakes are cool, take out the centers with an apple corer and fill each cupcake with a teaspoon of raspberry jelly. Replace core.

**8.** To glaze, heat ½ cup raspberry jelly in a small pan over low heat. Brush on cooled and filled cupcakes with a pastry brush. Make criss-cross patterns on top of each cupcake with either whipped cream or a decorator tube. Put a half hazelnut or almond in each square and dust with a little powdered sugar.

# MENDIANT Cupcakes with Fig Topping

The term "mendiant" generally means beggar in French, but in the kitchen it refers to preparations made with dried fruits and nuts. Use your favorite one.

**MAKES: ABOUT 16 REGULAR CUPCAKES OR 8 JUMBO CUPCAKES**

½ cup hazelnuts
½ cup almonds
2 cups all-purpose flour
2 teaspoons baking powder
1 teaspoon baking soda
1 teaspoon salt
1 teaspoon cinnamon
½ teaspoon allspice
½ cup/1 stick unsalted butter, room temperature
1 cup dark brown sugar, firmly packed
2 eggs
4 teaspoons white vinegar
⅔ cup milk
½ cup raisins

FIG TOPPING
2 cups dried figs
1½ cups water
1 cinnamon stick
¾ cup sugar

1. Place all of the topping ingredients in a heavy pan and bring to a boil. Lower heat and simmer for about 20 minutes or until the figs are tender and about half of the water has evaporated. Remove cinnamon stick and discard. Purée the fig mixture in a food processor. Set aside.

2. Preheat oven to 350°F. Put hazelnuts and almonds in a dish in the oven and cook them until they are browned, about 10 minutes, stirring from time to time. Keep a close eye on them as you don't want them to burn. You can do the same thing in a heavy pan on a burner. Coarsely grind the nuts in a food processor and set aside.

3. Mix flour, baking powder, baking soda, salt, and spices and set aside.

4. Cream butter and sugar until light and fluffy. Add eggs, one at a time, mixing well after each addition. Combine vinegar and milk. Alternately add dry ingredients and liquid, beating until smooth after each addition. Fold in raisins and ground nuts.

5. Spoon batter into regular or jumbo cupcake papers, filling cups just a little over ½ full. Cook for about 20 minutes, until just barely cooked. Remove from oven and spread fig mixture over each cupcake. Return to oven and cook for another 10 minutes or until cooked. Remove from oven and cool completely before unmolding.

# MARRAKECH Moments

I remember arriving in Marrakech at Christmas time with the orange trees heavy with fruit and the smell of orange flower blossom in the air. Thus, my inspiration for this dazzling duo.

**MAKES: ABOUT 12 CUPCAKES**

¾ cup cream cheese, softened
¼ cup sugar
2 tablespoons finely grated orange rind
1 tablespoon orange juice

CHOCOLATE BATTER
1½ cups all-purpose flour
2 teaspoons baking powder
1 teaspoon salt
1 cup sugar
⅓ cup unsweetened cocoa powder
½ cup milk
⅓ cup vegetable oil
1 egg
1 teaspoon vanilla extract

CHOCOLATE ORANGE GANACHE
6 ounces dark chocolate, broken into little pieces
¾ cup heavy cream
3 tablespoons orange liqueur (Cointreau, Grand Marnier, etc.)

FOR DECORATION
Orange sugar or grated orange rind
Candied orange

1. Preheat oven to 350°F. Mix the cream cheese, sugar, orange rind, and orange juice in a bowl and set aside.

2. In a large bowl, mix flour, baking powder, salt, sugar, and cocoa powder.

3. In a small bowl, mix milk, oil, egg, and vanilla. Pour liquid into flour mixture and beat well with a wooden spoon.

4. Put a heaping tablespoon of the chocolate batter in the bottom of 12 cupcake papers. Divide up the orange cream cheese batter among the cupcakes (about a heaping teaspoon per cupcake).

5. Spoon over the remaining chocolate batter. Gently swirl batter with a knife (don't overdo it). Bake for 25–30 minutes or until a tester inserted into the center comes out clean. Remove from oven and cool.

6. To make the ganache: place chocolate and cream in a double boiler or a microwave and heat until cream is warm to the touch and chocolate starts to melt. Remove from heat and stir until all of the chocolate has melted and the mixture is homogeneous. Remember, you don't want to cook the chocolate, you just want to melt it. You can always put it back over warm water or in the microwave for a few seconds if you need to. Stir in orange liqueur. Cool slightly then dip cupcakes in chocolate. The ganache will be smooth and shiny. Decorate with orange sugar or a piece of candied orange rind.

# PINEAPPLE Surprises

The origin of this cupcake is a dessert that we used to serve at our restaurant. We were looking for something easy to put together and discovered this one on a trip to Spain and then adapted it to our taste. It actually consists of a regular size cupcake, topped with a mini-cupcake (with a brandied cherry hidden inside) and decorated to look like a pineapple.

**MAKES: ABOUT 12 CUPCAKES**

1½ cups all-purpose flour
2 teaspoons baking powder
1 teaspoon salt
¾ cup/1½ sticks unsalted butter
1½ cups sugar
3 eggs
½ cup juice (drained from pineapple)
1 small can crushed pineapple, drained (about ½ cup)
½ cup shredded coconut
12 pitted brandied cherries or maraschino cherries

PINEAPPLE FONDANT GLAZE
1½ cups powdered sugar
2 tablespoons juice drained from pineapple
Yellow food coloring
Brown decorator frosting or caramel for decoration
Candied pineapple or pineapple candy for decoration

1. Preheat oven to 350°F.

2. Mix flour, baking powder, and salt together and set aside.

3. Cream butter and sugar until light and fluffy. Add eggs, one at a time, mixing well after each addition. Alternately add dry ingredients and pineapple juice. When batter is well blended, fold in pineapple and shredded coconut.

4. Spoon batter into 12 regular cupcake papers and 12 mini silicon molds, filling cups about ½ full. Bake regular cupcakes for about 20–25 minutes and mini-cupcakes for a shorter time, or until a tester inserted into the center comes out clean. Remove from oven and cool.

5. Turn cooled mini-cupcakes over and remove a little bit of the center. Replace it with a brandied cherry.

6. To make the glaze: mix powdered sugar and pineapple juice together until you obtain a smooth paste. Add yellow food coloring. Frost top of regular cupcakes. Place a mini-cupcake (with the cherry inside) on top while glaze is still soft. Ice. Decorate with brown decorator frosting or caramel to make the cupcake look like a pineapple. Place a piece of candied pineapple or a pineapple candy on top.

# MACADAMIA & WHITE CHOCOLATE Cupcakes

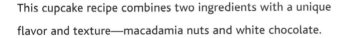

This cupcake recipe combines two ingredients with a unique flavor and texture—macadamia nuts and white chocolate.

**MAKES: ABOUT 12–14 CUPCAKES**

1½ cups all-purpose flour
2 teaspoons baking powder
1 teaspoon baking soda
1 teaspoon salt
½ cup/1 stick unsalted butter
¾ cup sugar
2 eggs
½ cup buttermilk
½ cup white chocolate chips
½ cup chopped macadamia nuts

**WHITE CHOCOLATE FROSTING**
4 ounces good quality white chocolate
¼ cup heavy cream
¾ cup cream cheese, room temperature
⅓ cup powdered sugar

FOR DECORATION
Macadamia nuts, whole
Grated white chocolate

1. Preheat oven to 350°F.

2. Mix flour, baking powder, baking soda, and salt together and set aside.

3. Cream butter and sugar until light and fluffy. Add eggs, one at a time, mixing well after each addition. Alternately add the dry ingredients and the liquid, beating until smooth after each addition. Fold in chocolate chips and macadamia nuts.

4. Spoon batter into cupcake papers, filling cups about ⅔ full. Bake for about 20–25 minutes or until a tester inserted into the center comes out clean. Remove from oven and cool.

5. To make the frosting: melt chocolate and cream in a double boiler or a microwave. Remove from heat when chocolate is just melted, stir and let cool. When mixture is cool to the touch, add cream cheese and powdered sugar. Beat until mixture is thick and creamy. Frost cooled cupcakes and decorate with macadamia nuts and grated white chocolate.

# ORIENT EXPRESS Cupcakes with Yin-Yang Frosting

East meets West in these lovely little green tea cupcakes. Enjoy them with a cup of green tea in the afternoon or for dessert after an Oriental-inspired meal.

**MAKES: ABOUT 12 CUPCAKES**

GREEN TEA CUPCAKE
1 cup all-purpose flour
1 teaspoon baking powder
½ teaspoon salt, plus pinch for the
  egg whites
2 teaspoons powdered Japanese
  green tea
2 eggs, separated
⅔ cup powdered sugar
½ cup ground almonds
6 tablespoons/¾ stick unsalted
  butter, room temperature, cut into
  little pieces
"YIN-YANG" FROSTING
See Midnight Sky Frosting (page 76)

1. Preheat oven to 350°F.

2. Mix flour, baking powder, salt, and tea together and set aside.

3. In a large bowl, beat egg yolks with powdered sugar until light in color. Add ground almonds and beat well. Add butter and blend until mixture is smooth. Add dry ingredients and mix well. Beat egg whites with a pinch of salt until stiff but not dry and gently fold into batter.

4. Spoon batter into cupcake papers, filling about ⅔ full. Bake for about 20 minutes or until a tester inserted into the center comes out clean. Remove from oven and cool.

5. Make the frosting according to the Midnight Sky Frosting recipe but before adding the black food coloring, divide the frosting into two bowls. Add black food coloring to one bowl and leave the other one white. Frost cooled cupcakes with a yin-yang design.

**CUPCAKE TIP**
*You can also frost the cupcakes with ready-made fondant or one of the fondant recipes on page 142. Another possibility would be to decorate the cupcakes with a Chinese character.*

# MINI-FINANCIER
## Cupcakes

A "financier," which literally means exactly that in French, is a small cake that is made with ground nuts and whipped egg whites. A dab of apricot jelly with some ground pistachios sprinkled on top and you will have a perfect accompaniment to a fruit salad or ice cream for dessert or a delicate finger cake for a 5 o'clock tea.

**MAKES: ABOUT 24–30 MINI-CUPCAKES**

1 cup all-purpose flour
1 teaspoon baking powder
½ teaspoon salt, plus pinch for the egg whites
½ cup finely ground almonds
1 cup light brown sugar
5 egg whites
½ cup/1 stick unsalted butter, melted and cooled
Several drops of almond extract
½ cup apricot jelly
½ cup ground pistachio nuts

**1.** Preheat oven to 350°F.

**2.** In a large bowl, combine the first five ingredients and set aside.

**3.** Beat egg whites with a pinch of salt until stiff but not dry. Fold into dry ingredients. Gradually add melted butter with a few drops of almond extract, gently folding it in with a whisk or a rubber spatula.

**4.** Spoon batter into mini-cupcake papers or silicon molds, filling just a little over ½ full. Bake for about 20 minutes or until a tester inserted in the center comes out clean. Remove from oven and cool.

**5.** In a small pan, melt apricot jelly until just warm. Add a few drops of water, if necessary. Brush the jelly on the cooled cupcakes with a pastry brush and sprinkle with ground pistachio nuts.

**CUPCAKE TIP**
*You can bake them either in mini-cupcake papers or in a silicon mini-cupcake mold.*

# POIRE Belle Helene

Here is another elegant French dessert transformed into a cupcake. A Poire Belle Hélène is usually vanilla ice cream served with a poached or ripe pear half and doused in chocolate sauce.

**MAKES: ABOUT 12 REGULAR CUPCAKES OR 6 JUMBO CUPCAKES**

1 cup all-purpose flour
1 teaspoon baking powder
½ teaspoon salt, plus pinch for the egg whites
7 ounces good quality dark chocolate (at least 55% cocoa solids)
½ cup/1 stick unsalted butter
⅔ cup sugar
3 eggs, separated
3 pears (fresh or canned), drained and cut into small pieces, plus 1 pear cut into lengthwise slices for decoration

CREAMY CHOCOLATE SAUCE
½ cup sugar
1 tablespoon all-purpose flour
Pinch of salt
1½ cups whole milk
3 ounces good quality dark chocolate (at least 55% cocoa solids), broken into pieces
2 tablespoons/¼ stick unsalted butter, cut into little pieces
1 teaspoon vanilla extract

1. Preheat oven to 350°F.

2. Mix flour, baking powder, and salt together and set aside.

3. Melt chocolate with butter in a double boiler or microwave. When just melted, remove from heat, stir well, and add sugar to chocolate mixture. Mix thoroughly. Add egg yolks, one by one, mixing well after each addition, followed by dry ingredients. Beat batter until smooth and all of the flour has disappeared.

4. Beat egg whites with pinch of salt until stiff but not dry. Gently fold into batter. Chop 2 pears into small pieces and carefully add to batter.

5. Spoon batter into cupcake papers, filling cups about ⅔ full. Bake for about 25 minutes or until a tester inserted into the center comes out clean. Remove from oven and cool.

6. To make the chocolate sauce (or use ready-made): in a small bowl, mix sugar, flour, and salt together and set aside.

7. Heat milk and chocolate in a heavy pan over low heat until just melted. Stir with a wooden spoon until smooth. Add dry ingredients to chocolate mixture, mixing well. Simmer for 5 minutes, stirring constantly. Remove from heat and stir in butter and vanilla.

8. Spoon warm chocolate sauce over cupcakes or dribble a little over the top of each cupcake and decorate with a slice of the remaining pear.

# WHITE CHOCOLATE & RASPBERRY Cupcakes

These easy and elegant cupcakes were inspired by a pie that a friend of mine once made with white chocolate, fresh raspberries, and decorated with real chocolate leaves.

**MAKES: ABOUT 12–14 CUPCAKES**

1⅓ cups all-purpose flour
1½ teaspoons baking powder
1 teaspoon salt
6 ounces white chocolate, broken up
  into little pieces
½ cup/1 stick unsalted butter, cut
  into little pieces
1 cup sugar
6 eggs
¾ cup dried raspberries

RASPBERRY BUTTER
CREAM FROSTING

1⅔ cups powdered sugar
1 cup/2 sticks unsalted butter, room
  temperature, cut into small pieces
Pinch of salt
2 tablespoons crème de framboise,
  raspberry liqueur or raspberry
  syrup
Chocolate leaves for decoration
  (see step 6)
Fresh or frozen raspberries for
  decoration

1. Preheat oven to 350°F.

2. Mix flour, baking powder, and salt together and set aside.

3. Melt chocolate and butter in a double boiler or a microwave. Remove from heat. Add sugar and mix well. Add eggs, one at a time, mixing well after each addition. Add dry ingredients. Fold in raspberries.

4. Spoon batter into cupcake papers, filling about ⅔ full. Bake for about 20–25 minutes or until a tester inserted into the center comes out clean. Remove from oven and cool.

5. To make the frosting: sift sugar into the large bowl of an electric mixer. Add butter and a pinch of salt. Beat on medium speed until frosting is light and fluffy. Add raspberry flavoring and continue beating until frosting is of good spreading consistency. Frost cooled cupcakes.

6. To make the chocolate leaves: melt about 8 ounces dark chocolate in a double boiler or microwave. Using a pastry brush, paint the undersides of leaves with the chocolate. You can use any nontoxic leaf (lemon or orange tree leaves). Place leaves on a piece of wax paper on a tray and put them in the refrigerator until chocolate has hardened (this will take only a few minutes). Very carefully peel off leaves.

7. Decorate frosted cupcakes with a few raspberries and chocolate leaves.

# GATEAU DE SAVOIE
# (Savoy Cake)

This cupcake is actually a very simple and basic sponge cake, that originated in the Savoy region of France, in the French Alps. The beauty of these cupcakes lies in their simplicity. You can add ½ cup of your favorite nuts or dried fruits, a few spoonfuls of coconut, a teaspoon of strong powdered espresso, etc. A very versatile cupcake, to say the least!

**MAKES: ABOUT 12 REGULAR CUPCAKES AND 24–30 MINI-CUPCAKES**

1 cup all-purpose flour
1 teaspoon baking powder
½ teaspoon salt, plus pinch for the egg whites
½ cup/1 stick unsalted butter, room temperature
¾ cup sugar
4 eggs, separated
1 teaspoon vanilla extract
Powdered sugar for dusting (optional)
Glaze or frosting of your choice

1. Preheat oven to 350°F.

2. Mix flour, baking powder, and salt together and set aside.

3. Cream butter with sugar until light and fluffy. Add egg yolks, one at a time, mixing well after each addition. Add the dry ingredients.

4. Beat egg whites with a pinch of salt until stiff but not dry. Gently fold into batter.

5. Spoon batter into cupcake papers, filling cups about ⅔ full. Bake for 20–25 minutes or until a tester inserted into the center comes out clean. Cupcakes should be elastic to the touch. Remove from oven and cool.

6. Dust the cooled cupcakes with powdered sugar, or glaze or frost them with the icing of your choice.

**CUPCAKE TIP**
*You can either frost them, glaze them, or dust them with powdered sugar and serve with a fruit salad.*

# SAFFRON & ORANGE
## Cupcakes

These gourmet cupcakes with their delicate saffron threads and subtle flavors of orange and almond will be the perfect accompaniment to a 5 o'clock cream tea. Serve them with a bowl of fresh cream and a mug of black tea and enjoy. You won't be hungry for dinner.

**MAKES: ABOUT 16–18 CUPCAKES**

2 cups freshly squeezed orange juice
1 tablespoons finely grated orange rind
¼ teaspoon saffron threads (not powder)
3 eggs
1 cup powdered sugar, plus more for dusting
1⅔ cups all-purpose flour
2 teaspoons baking powder
1 teaspoon salt
1½ cups ground almonds
½ cup/1 stick unsalted butter, melted

1. Preheat oven to 350°F.

2. In a medium pan, bring orange juice, orange rind, and saffron to a boil. Lower the heat and simmer for 1 minute. Remove from heat and cool.

3. In a large bowl, cream eggs and sugar until they are light and foamy. Add flour, baking powder, salt, almonds, orange juice mixture, and butter, mixing ingredients in rapidly with a wooden spoon. The mixture may be a little lumpy.

4. Spoon batter into cupcake papers, filling ⅔ full, and smoothing over with a spoon. Bake for about 25 minutes or until a tester inserted into the center comes out clean. Remove from oven and cool.

5. Dust with powdered sugar and serve with a bowl of thick fresh cream.

**CUPCAKE TIP**
*You can also frost these cupcakes if you prefer. Try one of the orange frostings (Fresh Orange Juice Frosting, page 137, for example) and decorate with Caramelized Slivered Almonds (page 87).*

# STRAWBERRY Cheesecakes

A cheesecake in a cupcake! Is it possible? Not really, but a little imagination will go a long way and no one will be disappointed after they have tasted these scrumptious, delectable morsels with a surprise inside and strawberries and cream on top. Let them eat cupcakes!

**MAKES: ABOUT 12 CUPCAKES**

3 tablespoons cream cheese
3/4 cup sugar
2 1/3 cups all-purpose flour
2 1/2 teaspoons baking powder
1 teaspoon salt
2 eggs, lightly beaten
1 cup milk
2 tablespoons/1/4 stick unsalted butter, melted
1 tablespoon finely grated orange rind
12 small strawberries, hulled and cleaned, for the filling

STRAWBERRIES AND CREAM FROSTING

1 egg white
Pinch of salt
1 cup heavy whipping cream
3/4 cup powdered sugar
2 tablespoons strawberry liqueur or strawberry syrup
1/2 cup strawberry purée

1. Preheat oven to 350°F.

2. Mix cream cheese with 1/4 cup sugar and set aside.

3. In a large bowl, mix flour, baking powder, salt, and the remaining 1/2 cup sugar.

4. In a separate bowl, beat eggs with milk and melted butter. Pour liquid into flour mixture and mix together rapidly with a wooden spoon. Blend in orange rind.

5. Put a heaping spoonful of the mixture into 12 cupcake papers (half the mixture). Place a strawberry and a teaspoonfull of the cream cheese in the center and cover with remaining mixture. Cook for 20 minutes in the oven. Remove and let cool before unmolding.

6. To make the frosting: beat egg white with salt until stiff but not dry. Beat whipping cream separately until it forms soft peaks, then slowly beat in the sugar and strawberry flavoring. Fold two mixtures together. Gently fold in puréed strawberries. Just before serving, heap the cream on the cupcakes and decorate to your taste.

# HOLIDAY
# CUPCAKES

# VALENTINE'S DAY Cupcakes

These filled cupcakes bring together one of the most divine duos known to chocolate lovers—chocolate and cherry—with a little cream thrown in for good measure.

**MAKES: ABOUT 16 CUPCAKES**

1½ cups all-purpose flour
½ cup unsweetened cocoa powder
2 teaspoons baking powder
1 teaspoon baking soda
1 teaspoon salt
½ cup/1 stick unsalted butter
1¼ cups sugar
2 eggs
1 teaspoon vanilla extract
⅔ cup sour cream

CHERRY CREAM CHEESE FILLING
¾ cup cream cheese
3 tablespoons sugar
4 tablespoons Maraschino cherry syrup
Maraschino cherries or pitted brandied cherries

CHERRY JUBILEE FROSTING
¼ cup/½ stick unsalted butter
2 cups powdered sugar
3 tablespoons Maraschino cherry syrup
Several drops red food coloring (optional)
Unsweetened cocoa powder (about 2 tablespoons) for dusting
Maraschino cherries for decoration

1. Preheat oven to 350°F.

2. Mix flour with cocoa, baking powder, baking soda, and salt. Set aside.

3. Cream butter and sugar until light and fluffy. Add eggs, one at a time, mixing well after each addition. Add vanilla. Alternately beat in flour mixture and sour cream.

4. Fill cupcake papers about ⅔ full. Bake for 25 minutes or until a tester inserted into the center comes out clean. Remove from oven and cool.

5. To make the filling: using a fork or in a blender or mixer, mix cream cheese, sugar, and cherry syrup together until smooth. You can use more syrup if necessary. Scoop out the center of each cupcake with an apple corer. Drop in a teaspoon of filling and a cherry. Replace core. Save leftover filling for frosting.

6. To make the frosting: cream butter with any leftover filling until light and fluffy. Add powdered sugar, cherry syrup, and food coloring and beat until smooth and creamy. Add more cherry syrup if necessary. Frost filled cupcakes. Lightly dust with cocoa and place a cherry on the top of each cupcake.

**CUPCAKE TIP**
*For a simpler alternative, use the Chocolate Fudge Icing for the Banana Split Cupcake (page 56).*

# ЄPIPHANЎ Cupcakes

The Feast of the Epiphany (also known as King's Day) celebrates the visit of the Three Wise Men to Bethlehem. In France today it is the unofficial ending of the holiday season.

**MAKES: ABOUT 12 CUPCAKES**

1¼ cups all-purpose flour
2 teaspoons baking powder
1 teaspoon salt
½ cup/1 stick unsalted butter
1⅛ cups sugar
3 eggs
½ cup milk
1 cup blanched almonds, finely chopped

ALMOND FILLING
½ cup almond paste, softened and cut into little pieces
⅓ cup cream cheese, room temperature
½ cup powdered sugar
12 jelly beans or Jordan almonds

ALMOND BUTTER CREAM FROSTING
6 tablespoons/¾ stick unsalted butter, room temperature
½ cup almond paste, softened and cut into little pieces
2½ cups powdered sugar
2 tablespoons milk
⅛ tsp almond extract
Jelly beans or Jordan almonds

1. To make filling: mix first three ingredients together (you can use a food processor, if necessary) and set aside. Preheat oven to 350°F.

2. Mix together flour, baking powder, and salt and set aside.

3. Cream butter and sugar together until light and fluffy. Add eggs, one at a time, mixing well after each addition. Alternately add dry ingredients and milk, beating until smooth. Fold in chopped almonds.

4. Fill 12 cupcake papers with half of the batter. Place a spoonful of filling in the center of the batter with a jelly bean or Jordan almond. Cover with remaining batter. Bake for about 20 minutes or until a tester inserted into the center comes out clean. Remove from oven and cool.

5. To make the frosting: cream butter and almond paste together until smooth (you can use a food processor, if necessary). Transfer to a large bowl, add sugar and beat until creamy. Gradually add milk and almond extract and continue beating. You can add a little extra milk for a softer frosting and more extract, if necessary.

6. Frost cooled cupcakes. Decorate with either jelly beans or Jordan almonds, three to a cupcake (for the Three Wise Men!). Alternatively, you can sprinkle the frosted cupcakes with caramelized slivered almonds (page 87). If you are using almond charms, be sure to warn your guests!

# ST. PATRICK'S DAY
## Pistachio Yogurt Cupcakes

St. Patrick's Day is marked by parades and fireworks, and symbolized by the shamrock, a three-leaved clover. So paint the town green with this little green gem of a cupcake.

**MAKES: ABOUT 18 CUPCAKES**

1 cup all-purpose flour
1 teaspoon baking powder
1 teaspoon baking soda
1 teaspoon salt
1 teaspoon ground cardamom
   (optional)
³/₄ cup/1¹/₂ sticks unsalted butter,
   room temperature
³/₄ cup brown sugar
3 eggs
1 teaspoon vanilla extract
¹/₂ cup whole yogurt
²/₃ cup unsalted pistachios, coarsely
   chopped (they can be roasted for
   more flavor)
Green food coloring (optional)

GREEN ICING
1 tablespoon unsalted butter, melted
2 tablespoons hot milk
1¹/₂ cups powdered sugar
Flavoring (optional)
Green food coloring

1. Preheat oven to 350°F.

2. Mix flour, baking powder, baking soda, salt, and ground cardamom together and set aside.

3. Cream butter and sugar until light and fluffy. Add eggs, one at a time, mixing well after each addition. Add vanilla and green food coloring, if using. Alternately beat in flour mixture and yogurt. Fold in pistachios.

4. Spoon batter into cupcake papers, filling cups about ²/₃ full. Bake for 25 minutes or until a tester comes out clean. Remove from oven and cool.

5. To make the icing: mix butter with hot milk in a large bowl. Slowly beat in sugar until the icing is of good spreading consistency. If you are using flavoring (almond, vanilla, etc.), add it now. Add green food coloring, drop by drop, until you obtain the desired color. Ice the cooled cupcakes and decorate to your taste.

**CUPCAKE TIP**
*You could decorate white iced cupcakes with orange sugar (for Northern Ireland) and green sugar (for the Republic of Ireland), with a white stripe down the middle representing hope for peace between them.*

# ST. PATRICK'S DAY IRISH SODA BREAD Cupcakes

The oatmeal, caraway seeds, and dried currants are typical of the traditional Irish recipe but this lighter version will definitely get you in the mood. Wash it down with a glass of Irish Whiskey or Bailey's Irish Cream and you may even see some leprechauns!

**MAKES: ABOUT 16 CUPCAKES**

2 cups all-purpose flour
1 tablespoon oatmeal
2 teaspoons baking powder
2 teaspoons baking soda
1 teaspoon salt
1/2 cup/1 stick unsalted butter, room temperature
1 cup sugar
2 eggs
3/4 cup buttermilk
1/2 cup dried currants or raisins
1 tablespon caraway seeds (optional)
IRISH WHISKEY FROSTING
1/4 cup/1/2 stick unsalted butter, room temperature
2 cups powdered sugar
Pinch of salt
2 tablespoons Irish whiskey (or Bailey's Irish Cream)
Green food coloring (optional)
Green sugar for sprinkling

1. Preheat oven to 350°F.

2. Mix dry ingredients together and set aside.

3. Cream butter and sugar until light and fluffy. Add eggs, one at a time, beating well after each addition. Alternately beat in flour mixture and buttermilk. Fold in currants or raisins and caraway seeds.

4. Spoon batter into cupcake papers, filling cups about 2/3 full. Bake for 25 minutes or until a tester inserted into the center comes out clean. Remove from oven and cool.

5. To make the frosting: cream butter, sugar, and salt until light and fluffy. Slowly add whiskey or Irish Cream (and food coloring, if you are using it) and beat until frosting is of good spreading consistency. Frost cooled cupcakes and sprinkle with green sugar.

**CUPCAKE TIP**
*For a simpler non-alcoholic version, just dust with powdered and green sugars.*

# MOTHER'S DAY FILLED ROSE
## Cupcakes

Say it with roses when you offer her these exquisitely delicate cupcakes made with rose water, filled with rose jelly, petals, and all, and topped with rose syrup frosting.

**MAKES: ABOUT 18 CUPCAKES**

2²/₃ cups all-purpose flour
3 teaspoons baking powder
1 teaspoon salt
½ cup /1 stick unsalted butter, room temperature
¼ cup sugar
2 eggs
¼ cup rose syrup
1 cup milk
Rose jelly

ROSE SYRUP FROSTING
6 tablespoons/¾ stick unsalted butter, room temperature
2 cups powdered sugar
3 tablespoons rose syrup
½ teaspoon rose water (optional)
Red food coloring (optional)

1. Preheat oven to 350°F.

2. Mix flour, baking powder, and salt together and set aside.

3. Cream butter and sugar until light and fluffy. Add eggs, one at a time, mixing well after each addition. Alternately add dry ingredients and syrup and milk to butter mixture, blending well after each addition.

4. Spoon batter into cupcake papers, filling cups about ²/₃ full. Bake for 25–30 minutes or until a tester inserted into the center comes out clean. Remove from oven and cool.

5. When cupcakes are cool, take the center out of each cupcake, using an apple corer. Drop a scant teaspoon of rose jelly into the center and replace cupcake core.

6. To make the frosting: cream butter with sugar until it is light and fluffy. Gradually add rose syrup, rose water, and food coloring, beating continually until frosting is of good spreading consistency. Frost cooled cupcakes and decorate to your taste.

# EASTER LEMON CHIFFON Cupcakes

Use bright Easter colors and decorate theses cupcakes as if they were Easter eggs, using colored sugars, little candies, stencils etc. Have the kids pitch in and decorate their own.

**MAKES: ABOUT 18 CUPCAKES**

½ cup all-purpose flour, sifted
Finely grated rind of 1 small lemon
6 egg whites
Pinch of salt or ½ teaspoon cream of tartar
1 cup sugar

EASTER EGG ICING

1 pound ready-to-use fondant or use one of the Fondant recipes (page 142)—if using the white meringue fondant, thin it with a little milk or sugar syrup
Sugar syrup (if required)
Food coloring

FOR DECORATION

Colored sugars
Easter motifs

1. Preheat oven to 350°F. Mix flour and lemon rind and set aside.

2. Put the egg whites, salt, or cream of tartar in a large bowl. Beat egg whites until stiff but not dry. You want them to be a little moist.  Beat in sugar, little by little.  Gradually fold in flour with a whisk.  This is the only time I ever sift flour.  It allows me to add it slowly and not to deflate the egg whites. Do not overmix. The batter will be just gorgeous —like a meringue.

3. Spoon batter into cupcake papers using two soup spoons, filling a little over half way. Cook for about 15–20 minutes until cupcakes are golden on top and spring back to the touch. Remove from oven and cool.

4. Prepare ready-to-use fondant, according to manufacturer's instructions, or one of the fondant recipes. This will probably require heating the fondant, either in a microwave or in a double boiler, until just melted. Overheating will spoil the glossy appearance and change the texture. Add enough sugar syrup to achieve the desired consistency. Pour the fondant into separate bowls, depending on the number of colors you wish to use. Add food coloring until you have obtained the desired color. Either dip cupcakes into the fondant or ice using a knife. Decorate with colored sugars and Easter motifs.

# EASTER LAVENDER BUTTERFLY Cupcakes

A bouquet of flowers in a cupcake—lavender, poppy, rose, and, with a little bit of
luck, violet! Easter is the holiday that we all associate with the beginning of spring,
so offer your friends and family a bouquet of flowers—with a butterfly on top.

**MAKES: ABOUT 24–30 CUPCAKES**

1⅓ cups all-purpose flour
2 teaspoons baking powder
1 teaspoon salt
½ cup/1 stick unsalted butter, room
   temperature
¾ cup sugar
2 eggs
1 teaspoon vanilla extract
½ cup light cream
2 tablespoons dried lavender flowers
2 tablespoons poppyseeds for
   decoration
Several teaspoons of your favorite
   jelly (strawberry, raspberry, etc.)
FILLING
1 cup heavy whipping cream, chilled
4 tablespoons sugar
½ teaspoon lemon extract or another
   flavoring
1 tablespoon grated lemon rind (if
   using lemon extract)

1. Preheat oven to 350°F.

2. Mix flour, baking powder, and salt together and set aside.

3. Cream butter and sugar until light and fluffy. Add eggs, one at a time,
mixing well after each addition, followed by vanilla. Alternately beat in
flour mixture and cream. Fold in lavender flowers.

4. Fill cupcake papers about ⅔ full. Bake for about 25 minutes or until
a tester inserted into the center comes out clean. Remove from oven
and cool.

5. To make the filling: in a large bowl, beat whipping cream. When it starts
to stiffen, gradually add sugar and beat until stiff peaks form. Add
flavoring and lemon rind.

6. Cut off the top of each cupcake and set aside—this will be the
butterfly. Using a sharp knife, carefully remove a little cone from the
center of each cupcake and fill with cream. Sprinkle with a few
poppyseeds. Cut the top in half and place the halves on top of the cream
to look like the wings of a butterfly. Put a little jelly in between the two
halves to look like the butterfly's body.

# JULY 4TH RED VELVET
## Cupcakes

It is hard to imagine why anyone would have thought of adding red food coloring to chocolate cake, but the final effect is quite dazzling—especially with a Red, White, and Blue theme.

**MAKES: ABOUT 18 REGULAR CUPCAKES OR 9 JUMBO CUPCAKES**

2 cups all-purpose flour
2 tablespoons unsweetened cocoa powder
2 teaspoons baking powder
1 teaspoon baking soda
1 teaspoon salt
½ cup/1 stick unsalted butter, room temperature
1½ cups sugar
2 eggs
1 teaspoon vanilla extract
1 teaspoon distilled white vinegar
1 tablespoon red food coloring
1 cup buttermilk
AMERICAN PARFAIT ICING
4 ounces white vegetable shortening (you can replace the shortening with butter but the icing won't be quite as "white")
1 tablespoon milk
½ teaspoon vanilla extract
1⅔ cups powdered sugar

1. Preheat oven to 350°F.

2. Mix flour, cocoa, baking powder, baking soda, and salt together and set aside.

3. Cream butter and sugar together until light and fluffy. Add eggs, one at a time, mixing well after each addition. Blend in vanilla, vinegar, and food coloring. Alternately add flour mixture and buttermilk and beat until batter is smooth.

4. Spoon batter into cupcake papers, filling about ⅔ full, and cook for 20–30 minutes or until a tester inserted into the center comes out clean. Remove from oven and cool.

5. To make the icing: cream shortening with milk until it is creamy. Add vanilla. Gradually add sugar to shortening. Beat with an electric mixer until icing is pale, light, and fluffy. You may need to add a little more milk to reach the desired consistency. Ice cooled cupcakes and decorate with colored sugars, stencils, sparklers, etc.

**CUPCAKE TIP**
*This icing is perfect for stencils and colored sugars.*

# JULY 4TH BLUEBERRY & RASPBERRY Cupcakes

These red, white, and blue cupcakes will warm a patriot's heart and a gourmet's stomach! Decorate them with fresh blueberries and raspberries, covered with a raspberry glaze, on a background of white fondant.

**MAKES: ABOUT 12 REGULAR CUPCAKES OR 6 JUMBO**

1⅔ cups all-purpose flour
2 teaspoons baking powder
1 teaspoon baking soda
1 teaspoon salt
½ cup/1 stick unsalted butter, room temperature
⅔ cup sugar
1 egg
1 cup buttermilk
1 teaspoon vanilla extract
½ cup blueberries (fresh or frozen)
½ cup raspberries (fresh or frozen)
Powdered sugar or white fondant glaze (see method)
½ cup raspberry jelly for glaze
Raspberries and blueberries for decoration

1. Preheat oven to 350°F.

2. Mix flour, baking powder, baking soda, and salt together and set aside.

3. Cream butter and sugar until light and fluffy. Add egg, buttermilk, and vanilla and mix well. Stir in dry ingredients. Gently fold in the blueberries and raspberries. If you are using frozen fruit, don't defrost before using.

4. Spoon batter into cupcake papers, filling about ⅔ full. Bake for about 25 minutes or until the top of the cupcakes are golden brown. Remove cupcakes from oven. Cool completely before unmolding.

5. Dust cooled cupcakes with powdered sugar or frost cooled cupcakes with White Fondant Glaze (page 142) or ready-to-use fondant.

6. After cupcakes are frosted, heat raspberry jelly in a small pan until it is just liquid (do not cook). Remove from heat immediately. Place a few raspberries in the center of the cupcakes (preferably while the fondant is still soft). Surround with blueberries. Using a pastry brush, apply raspberry jelly to fruits. This will make them shiny and will hold them in place after glaze has cooled.

# THANKSGIVING CARROT & CRANBERRY Cupcakes

These can be served as a dessert, as an alternative to pumpkin pie, after a Thanksgiving feast, and will be a welcome treat to kids and adults alike throughout the harvest season.

**MAKES: ABOUT 12 CUPCAKES**

1 cup all-purpose flour
1 teaspoon baking powder
1 teaspoon salt
2 teaspoons cinnamon
$\frac{1}{2}$ teaspoon grated nutmeg
$\frac{1}{2}$ cup vegetable oil
$\frac{1}{2}$ cup sugar
$\frac{1}{4}$ cup brown sugar, packed
2 eggs
1 cup grated carrots
$\frac{1}{2}$ cup walnuts, chopped
$\frac{1}{2}$ cup dried cranberries

CINNAMON AND SPICE FROSTING
$\frac{1}{4}$ cup/$\frac{1}{2}$ stick unsalted butter
$\frac{3}{4}$ cup/9 oz cream cheese
1 cup powdered sugar
1 teaspoon vanilla extract
1 teaspoon cinnamon
$\frac{1}{2}$ teaspoon ground ginger
$\frac{1}{2}$ teaspoon grated nutmeg
$\frac{1}{4}$ teaspoon ground cloves
Cinnamon for dusting
Candy corn for decoration

1. Preheat oven to 350°F.

2. Mix flour, baking powder, salt, and spices together and set aside.

3. Using an electric mixer or a wooden spoon, beat oil and both sugars until blended. Add eggs, one at a time, and beat until smooth. Add flour mixture and blend thoroughly. Fold in carrots, walnuts, and cranberries.

4. Fill cupcake papers about $\frac{2}{3}$ full. Bake for 25–30 minutes or until a tester inserted into the center comes out clean. Remove from oven and cool.

5. To make the frosting: cream butter and cream cheese together until light and fluffy. Gradually add powdered sugar, beating until smooth. Add vanilla and spices and continue beating until frosting is of good spreading consistency. Frost cooled cupcakes, dust with cinnamon, and decorate with candy corn.

**CUPCAKE TIP**
*Fresh or frozen cranberries could be used as well.*

# THANKSGIVING APPLE CIDER Cupcakes

This cupcake is a perfect fall dessert or snack. The cider gives the batter a certain lightness but if you prefer a non-alcoholic version, just use apple juice.

**MAKES: ABOUT 12 CUPCAKES**

1½ cups all-purpose flour
2 teaspoons baking powder
1 teaspoon salt
1 teaspoon cinnamon
½ cup/1 stick unsalted butter, room temperature
⅔ cup sugar
2 eggs
¾ cup hard cider
1 cup dried apples, cut into little pieces

APPLE FILLING
2½ cups apples, peeled, cored, and chopped into small pieces (about 3–4 apples)
1 cup light brown sugar
6 tablespoons/¾ stick unsalted butter, cut into small pieces
⅛ cup water
1 teaspoon cinnamon
½ teaspoon salt
Cinnamon for dusting
Apple wedges (either dried or fresh)

1. Preheat oven to 350°F.

2. Mix flour, baking powder, salt, and cinnamon together and set aside.

3. Cream butter and sugar together until light and fluffy. Add eggs, one at a time, blending well after each addition. Alternately add cider and dry ingredients. When batter is thoroughly blended, fold in dried apples.

4. Spoon batter into cupcake papers, filling cups about ⅔ full. Bake for about 25 minutes or until a tester inserted into the center comes out clean. Remove from oven and cool.

5. When cupcakes are cool, scoop out the center and heap full with Apple Filling or apple sauce. You can make your own or use the store-bought version. To make your own: combine all filling ingredients in a heavy pan and cook over low heat for about 5–10 minutes or until apples are soft. Remove from heat and crush apples with a fork. Cool before filling cupcakes.

6. Dust each cupcake with a little cinnamon and top with an apple wedge.

**CUPCAKE TIP**
*Save the cupcake centers and freeze them. They will make wonderful Lamingtons (see recipe on page 178)*

# HALLOWEEN ORANGE JUICE Cupcakes

Orange juice is one of the main ingredients in both the cupcake and the frosting, so it will be both beautiful and healthy! The lovely orange glaze lends itself marvelously well to Halloween decorations—colored sugars, stencils, etc.

**MAKES: ABOUT 16 CUPCAKES**

2 cups all-purpose flour
2 teaspoons baking powder
1 teaspoon salt
½ cup/1 stick unsalted butter, room
    temperature
1 cup sugar
2 eggs
Juice and finely grated rind of
    1 orange
1 tablespoon lemon juice
A few drops orange food coloring
    (optional)

ORANGE DECORATOR GLAZE
1 cup sugar
¼ cup cornstarch
1 cup orange juice (fresh, if possible)
1 teaspoon lemon juice
Pinch of salt
2 tablespoons/¼ stick unsalted
    butter
Orange food coloring (optional)

1. Preheat oven to 350°F. Mix flour, baking powder, and salt and set aside.

2. Cream butter and sugar until light and fluffy. Add eggs, one at a time, mixing well after each addition.

3. Combine orange juice and lemon juice and add enough water to make ⅔ cup. Alternately add flour mixture and liquid. Add orange rind and beat batter until smooth. Add food coloring if you are using it.

4. Spoon batter into cupcake papers, filling cups about ⅔ full. Bake for 25 minutes or until a tester inserted into the center comes out clean. Remove from oven and cool.

5. To make the glaze: combine sugar and cornstarch in a pan over low heat. Gradually add orange and lemon juices and stir until well blended. Add salt and butter. Cook over low heat, stirring constantly until the mixture is thick and glossy. Remove from heat and cool. Add food coloring, if desired. Glaze the cooled cupcakes. Decorate with Halloween colors and themes.

# HALLOWEEN PUMPKIN PECAN Cupcakes

This is a pumpkin pie in a cupcake. Offer them to trick-or-treaters when they come to your door or serve them at a Halloween party.

**MAKES: ABOUT 16 CUPCAKES**

1²/₃ cups all-purpose flour
2 teaspoons baking powder
1 teaspoon salt
1 teaspoon cinnamon
¹/₂ teaspoon ground ginger
¹/₂ teaspoon grated nutmeg
¹/₄ teaspoon ground cloves
¹/₂ cup/1 stick unsalted butter, room
   temperature
³/₄ cup brown sugar
2 eggs
2 teaspoons vanilla extract
1 cup cooked or canned pumpkin
1 cup chopped pecans (or any type of
   nut, raisins, or mini-marshmallows)

FRESH ORANGE JUICE FROSTING
¹/₄ cup/¹/₂ stick unsalted butter, room
   temperature
2 cups powdered sugar
1 tablespoon fresh orange juice
1 tablespoon grated orange rind
1 egg white
Pinch of salt

1. Preheat oven to 350°F.

2. Mix flour, baking powder, salt, and spices together and set aside.

3. Cream butter and sugar until light and fluffy. Add eggs, one at a time, mixing well after each addition. Add vanilla and pumpkin and beat until smooth. Add dry ingredients. Fold in pecans.

4. Spoon batter into cupcake papers, filling cups about ²/₃ full. Smooth batter with the back of a spoon. Bake for 30 minutes or until a tester inserted into the center comes out clean. Remove from oven and cool completely before unmolding.

5. To make the frosting: cream butter and sugar until light and fluffy. Add orange juice and rind and continue beating. Beat egg white with a pinch of salt until stiff but not dry. Gently fold into mixture. Spread on cooled cupcakes and decorate to your taste.

**CUPCAKE TIP**
*The orange frosting can be left as is or decorated for the occasion with a piece of candied orange peel or pumpkin seeds, colored sugars, black decorator frosting, etc.*

# DAY OF THE DEAD CHOC CINNAMON Cupcakes

"Dia de los Muertos" is a festive Mexican event to honor the dead, celebrated in November. This recipe calls for typical Mexican chocolate (mixed with cinnamon and raw sugar).

**MAKES: ABOUT 16 CUPCAKES**

1¾ cups all-purpose flour
2 teaspoons baking powder
1 teaspoon salt, plus pinch for the
   egg whites
1 teaspoon cinnamon
6 ounces/2 disks Mexican chocolate
½ cup milk
½ cup/1 stick unsalted butter, room
   temperature
¾ cup brown sugar
4 eggs, separated
1 teaspoon vanilla extract (Mexican,
   if possible)

CINNAMON BUTTER FROSTING
½ cup/1 stick unsalted butter
2 cups powdered sugar
1 tablespoon milk
1 teaspoon vanilla extract (Mexican,
   if possible)
1 teaspoon cinnamon

FOR DECORATION
Cinnamon or green and red sugars
Skulls and crossbones
Cinnamon candies

1. Preheat oven to 350°F. Mix dry ingredients together and set aside.

2. Melt chocolate and milk together in a double boiler or a microwave. As soon as the chocolate is melted, remove from heat, stir to blend, set aside, and cool.

3. Cream butter and brown sugar until light and fluffy. Add egg yolks, one at a time, mixing well after each addition. Add chocolate mixture and vanilla and mix until completely blended. Add flour mixture in three parts, blending well until flour disappears.

4. Beat egg whites with a pinch of salt until they are stiff but not dry. Gently fold whites into batter. Spoon batter into cupcake papers, filling cups about ⅔ full. Cook for about 20–25 minutes or until a tester inserted into the center comes out clean.

5. To make the frosting: cream butter and sugar until light and fluffy. Add milk, vanilla, and cinnamon and continue beating until frosting is of a good spreading consistency. Spread over cooled cupcakes and decorate.

6. To decorate: sprinkle with cinnamon or green and red sugars (the color of the Mexican flag), skulls and crossbones, marigolds, little cinnamon candies, etc. Day of the Dead sugar heads can be found in Mexican specialty stores and are a great item besides being a beautiful decoration.

# CHANUKAH HONEY HAZELNUT Cupcakes

Chanukah is the Jewish Festival of Lights and one of the most joyous holidays of the Jewish calender. These delicate hazelnut cupcakes will add a gourmet touch to that very ungourmet but oh-so-delicious traditional Chanukah meal of potato latkes with sour cream and applesauce.

**MAKES: ABOUT 12 CUPCAKES**

10 tablespoons/1¼ sticks unsalted butter, cut into pieces
½ cup honey
¼ cup all-purpose flour
¾ cup sugar
½ cup powdered or ground hazelnuts
1 teaspoon salt, plus pinch for the egg whites
4 eggs, separated
HONEY GLAZE
2 tablespoons honey
1 tablespoon fresh lemon juice
½ cup powdered sugar, plus more for dusting (optional)
Candies (optional) for decoration

1. Preheat oven to 350°F.

2. Melt butter and honey together in a pan and set aside.

3. Mix flour, sugar, hazelnuts, and salt in a bowl and set aside.

4. Beat egg whites with a pinch of salt until stiff but not dry. Set aside.

5. Pour butter and honey into dry ingredients and stir vigorously with a wooden spoon. Add egg yolks and mix well. Gently fold in egg whites. Batter will be light and airy.

6. Spoon batter into 12 cupcake papers, filling a little over ½ full. Cook for 20–25 minutes or until a tester inserted into the center comes out clean. Remove from oven and cool.

7. To make the glaze: heat honey in a small pan until it is just warm. Gradually add honey and lemon juice to sugar, stirring to blend. Spread on cooled cupcakes and let cool. Place a candle in the center of each cupcake before serving. Alternatively, dust the cooled cupcakes with powdered sugar.

# CHRISTMAS PEPPERMINT CHOCOLATE Cupcakes

These Christmas cupcakes will definitely evoke unforgettable visions of candy canes. Serve them as part of a Christmas buffet and throughout the holiday season.

**MAKES: ABOUT 18 CUPCAKES**

1 cup water
4 peppermint tea bags
2 cups all-purpose flour
2 teaspoons baking powder
1 teaspoon baking soda
1 teaspoon salt, plus pinch for the egg whites
3 ounces dark chocolate
1½ cups sugar
½ cup/1 stick unsalted butter, cut into small pieces
2 eggs, separated
½ cup sour cream or buttermilk

PEPPERMINT CANDY FROSTING
½ cup cream cheese, softened
1 tablespoon milk
Pinch of salt
A few drops of mint extract
2½ cups powdered sugar
¼ cup crushed peppermint candies or sticks
Miniature peppermint candy canes or green and red sugar for decoration

1. Preheat oven to 350°F.

2. Boil water in a small pan and add tea bags. Let steep for about 10 minutes. Remove tea bags and discard.

3. While tea is steeping, mix flour, baking powder, baking soda, and salt together and set aside.

4. In the top of a double boiler, over simmering water, place mint tea, chocolate, sugar, and butter. Stir until chocolate and butter have melted and mixture is smooth (you can use a microwave, if you prefer). Remove from heat and whisk in egg yolks, beating well. Alternately add flour mixture and sour cream or buttermilk and beat until batter is smooth.

5. Beat egg whites with a pinch of salt until they are stiff but not dry and gently fold into batter.

6. Spoon batter into cupcake papers, filling cups about ⅔ full. Bake for 25 minutes or until a tester inserted into the center comes out clean. Remove from oven and cool.

7. To make the frosting: in a large bowl, blend cream cheese, milk, salt, and mint extract and beat well. Gradually blend in powdered sugar until smooth and creamy. Fold in crushed candy. Spread on cooled cupcakes and decorate with a miniature candy cane and green and red sugar.

# CHRISTMAS FRUIT
## Cupcakes with White Fondant

These cupcakes are a cross between a Christmas pudding and a fruit cake, with a dash of brandy to warm your heart on a cold Christmas Eve.

**MAKES: ABOUT 12 REGULAR CUPCAKES OR 6 JUMBO CUPCAKES**

1 cup candied fruits
⅓ cup brandy
2 cups all-purpose flour
⅔ cup light brown sugar
2 teaspoons baking powder
1 teaspoon salt
1 teaspoon allspice
1 teaspoon ground cinnamon
½ teaspoon ground ginger
½ teaspoon grated nutmeg
½ cup milk
1 egg, slightly beaten
2 tablespoons apricot jelly
1 teaspoon finely grated orange rind
1 teaspoon finely grated lemon rind
½ cup/1 stick unsalted butter, melted
   and cooled

WHITE FONDANT GLAZE
1 cup powdered sugar
1 teaspoon finely grated lemon rind
1 tablespoon lemon juice

1. In a bowl, mix fruits and brandy and let stand for about 2 hours, stirring from time to time.

2. Preheat oven to 350°F.

3. In a large bowl, mix flour, sugar, baking powder, salt, and spices together and set aside.

4. Lightly beat the milk with the egg, apricot jelly, orange and lemon rinds, and melted butter. Add to flour mixture and mix well. Stir in fruits and brandy.

5. Spoon batter into cupcake papers, filling about ⅔ full, and cook for 20–30 minutes, or until a tester inserted into the center comes out clean. Remove from oven and cool.

6. To make the fondant glaze: mix powdered sugar and lemon rind together and gradually add lemon juice until you obtain a smooth paste, easy to spread. You may not need all of the lemon juice. Glaze and decorate cupcakes to your taste.

**CUPCAKE TIP**
*You can use either the fondant glaze recipe or ready-to use fondant.*

# NEW YEAR'S EVE PINK CHAMPAGNE Cupcakes

There's nothing like champagne to usher out the old year and bring in the new one! Top these light and delicious cupcakes with a champagne popper and welcome in the New Year in style.

**MAKES: ABOUT 16 CUPCAKES**

2 cups all-purpose flour
2 teaspoons baking powder
½ teaspoon salt
½ cup/1 stick unsalted butter, room temperature
1½ cups sugar
¾ cup pink champagne
Red food coloring (optional)
6 egg whites
Pinch of salt or cream of tartar
CHAMPAGNE FROSTING
¾ cup/1½ sticks unsalted butter, room temperature
2 cups powdered sugar
2 tablespoons champagne
Red food coloring (optional)
Mini champagne poppers for decoration

1. Preheat oven to 350°F.

2. Mix dry ingredients together and set aside.

3. Cream butter and sugar until light and fluffy. Alternately beat in flour mixture and champagne, blending well after each addition. Add food coloring, if desired.

4. Beat egg whites with a pinch of salt or cream of tartar until stiff but not dry and gently fold into batter.

5. Fill cupcake papers about ⅔ full. Bake for 25–30 minutes or until a tester inserted into the center comes out clean. Remove from oven and cool.

6. To make the frosting: beat butter and sugar until soft and creamy. Slowly add champagne and red food coloring, if desired and continue beating until frosting is of good spreading consistency. You can add more champagne for a softer frosting. Frost cooled cupcakes and decorate with a champagne popper.

**CUPCAKE TIP**
*If you prefer not to use alcohol, you can use cherry or strawberry soda instead of champagne to obtain the same effect.*

# NEW YEAR'S EVE CONFETTI Cupcakes

Welcome the New Year in with confetti. The crushed candies in the cupcakes will look like confetti when you bite in to them.

**MAKES: ABOUT 12 REGULAR CUPCAKES OR 24 MINI-CUPCAKES**

1 cup all-purpose flour
1 teaspoon baking powder
1 teaspoon salt
6 tablespoons/¾ stick unsalted
   butter, room temperature
½ cup sugar
3 eggs
1 tablespoon brandy or 1 teaspoon
   vanilla extract
⅓ cup light cream or half-and-half
½ cup crushed mints or hard candies
   of different colors

4-MINUTE CONFETTI FROSTING

1 egg white
¾ cup sugar
Pinch of salt
3 tablespoons water
1 teaspoon light corn syrup
1 teaspoon vanilla extract or
   1 tablespoon brandy
Candy confetti (can be found in the
   baking section of grocery stores)

1. Preheat oven to 350°F.

2. Mix flour, baking powder, and salt together and set aside.

3. Cream butter and sugar until light and fluffy. Add eggs, one at a time, mixing well after each addition, followed by brandy or vanilla. Alternately beat in flour mixture and cream or half-and-half. Fold in crushed candies.

4. Fill cupcake papers about ⅔ full. Bake for about 20 minutes or until a tester inserted into the center comes out clean. Remove from oven and cool.

5. To make the frosting: place egg white, sugar, salt, water, and corn syrup in a double boiler. Beat for about 1 minute until thoroughly mixed. Place over boiling water and beat at high speed for about 4 minutes or until frosting forms stiff peaks. Remove from heat and transfer to a large bowl. Add vanilla or brandy and beat for another minute or until of good spreading consistency. Frost cooled cupcakes and sprinkle candy confetti over cupcakes before frosting hardens.

# CUPCAKES
## PLUS

# DESSERT ROSE
## Cupcakes

I originally put this "cupcake" in the Kids section since it will certainly be a great favorite with them. But after writing the introduction to this book, I realized that it really doesn't fit my "strict" definition of a cupcake so I moved it here. It doesn't require any cooking and can be made with little or no help from an adult. It is perfect for a party or just a snack and can be whipped up in the blink of an eye. The kids will love this one!

**MAKES: ABOUT 12 REGULAR CUPCAKES OR 24 MINI-CUPCAKES**

8 ounces milk or dark chocolate, broken into pieces
¾ cup/1½ sticks unsalted butter, room temperature, cut into pieces
1⅓ cups powdered sugar
2 cups corn flakes

**1.** Melt chocolate and butter in a double boiler or a microwave oven. Mix well.

**2.** Stir in powdered sugar. Add corn flakes and mix gently until all of the corn flakes are coated with chocolate.

**3.** Spoon mixture into mini- or regular cupcake papers and set in the refrigerator for a few hours. Remove from refrigerator and enjoy.

**CUPCAKE TIP**
*You can replace the milk or dark chocolate with white chocolate and the corn flakes with Rice Krispies, Special K, or similar types of breakfast cereals.*

# ALMOND & HAZELNUT
## Mini-Meringues

These mini-meringues are made in mini-silicon cupcake molds. They can be eaten as is, served with fruit salad or ice cream or used with other desserts. They are easy to make and versatile in addition to being absolutely delicious.

**MAKES: ABOUT 30 MINI-MERINGUES CUPCAKES**

½ cup ground almonds
½ cup ground hazelnuts
¾ cup sugar
5 egg whites
Pinch of salt
¾ cup hazelnuts or almonds, toasted and coarsely chopped
Powdered sugar for dusting

**CUPCAKE TIP**
*They can be kept at room temperature for several days in a sealed container or frozen for future use.*

**1.** Preheat oven to 325°F.

**2.** Mix ground almonds, ground hazelnuts, and ¼ cup of the sugar together. Set aside. If you prefer, you can use just almonds, just hazelnuts, or any combination of either.

**3.** Beat egg whites with salt until they turn opaque. Gradually add remaining sugar and continue to beat whites until they are stiff and form glossy peaks. Gently fold in ground nut mixture, using a whisk or a rubber spatula. I start with the whisk and finish with the spatula. Take care not to overmix.

**4.** Fill the mini-cupcake molds with the mixture. You can use a pastry bag to do this if you wish but if not, just heap the mixture into the molds. Sprinkle the toasted nuts over the mini-meringues, pressing them in gently. Lightly dust with powdered sugar. Let the meringues rest for 10 minutes and then dust them again with powdered sugar and let them rest another 10 minutes.

**5.** Bake for about 25–30 minutes or until they are golden brown and firm to the touch. Cool before unmolding.

# DEEP-DISH APPLE PIE
## Cupcakes

Deep-Dish Apple Pie is an all-American favorite and for good reason. These cupcakes work particularly well in silicon molds, either the regular or jumbo version. Serve them on individual plates with a wedge of sharp cheddar cheese or a dollop of whipped cream.

**MAKES: ABOUT 8 REGULAR CUPCAKES OR 4 JUMBO CUPCAKES**

PIE DOUGH
See Chocolate Cupcake Pie (page 152)

APPLE PIE FILLING
3 cups apples, peeled, cored, and cut into pieces
1 tablespoon lemon juice
$\frac{1}{2}$ cup, plus 2 tablespoons sugar
Pinch of salt
Dash of grated nutmeg
1 teaspoon cinnamon
2 tablespoons all-purpose flour
2 tablespoons/$\frac{1}{4}$ stick unsalted butter, room temperature

1. Preheat oven to 450°F.

2. See Chocolate Cupcake Pie (page 152) for instructions on rolling out pie dough and lining molds. Serve enough dough to cut circles to cover the cupcakes.

3. In a large bowl, toss apples with lemon juice, $\frac{1}{2}$ cup sugar, salt, nutmeg, cinnamon, and flour, coating evenly. Scoop mixture into pie shells and dot with butter. Cover each cupcake with a circle of dough, crimping the edges for a pretty effect. Cut two vents into the top of each cupcake so that the steam can escape and sprinkle with remaining sugar.

4. Bake in the oven for 10 minutes and then turn down heat to 350°F. Cook for another 15–20 minutes or until pie crust is golden brown. Cool cupcakes completely before removing from molds.

VARIATION: DEEP-DISH PEACH PIE CUPCAKE
Substitute peaches for apples and cut into slices. Use just a pinch of cinnamon.

VARIATION: DEEP-DISH BLUEBERRY PIE CUPCAKE
Substitute blueberries for apples. Leave out cinnamon.

# CHOCOLATE
## Cupcake Pies

The inspiration for this cupcake was a pie that I used to make for my restaurant, itself inspired by a recipe from Bernachon, the great "chocolatier" from Lyon. When I was testing the recipe, I just naturally assumed that I would have to use silicon molds but my experiments proved that it was possible to make the cupcakes in cupcake papers as well.

**MAKES: ABOUT 14–16 CUPCAKES**

PIE DOUGH
Enough pie dough (any type—basic, flaky, etc.), homemade or ready-made to make two 9-inch pies.
All-purpose flour for dusting

CHOCOLATE FILLING
4 ounces good quality dark chocolate, broken into small pieces
2 cups liquid whole cream
²/₃ cup sugar
5 eggs

FOR DECORATION
Walnut halves (optional)
Whipped cream (optional)

1. Preheat oven to 350°F.

2. Roll out the pie dough on a lightly floured surface and cut out circles measuring 4 inches in diameter. Line silicon cupcake molds or cupcake papers, folding the edge of the dough back under so that it will look pretty. Make a few holes in the bottom of the dough so that it doesn't buckle when cooked. Be gentle!

3. Melt chocolate in a double boiler or a microwave. Remove from heat as soon as it is melted (do not cook). Add cream, sugar, and eggs and beat until all of the ingredients are totally blended.

4. Carefully pour chocolate mixture into pie shells, filling about ³/₄ full. Bake for about 25 minutes or until chocolate is cooked. The filling will rise while cooking but will fall when it cools. Cool cupcakes completely before removing from molds.

5. Decorate with a walnut half or a dollop of whipped cream, or both. If you are making the cupcakes in the silicon molds, serve them in pretty cupcake papers.

# CHERRY ALMOND PIE Cupcakes

Although you can use just about any filling for pie cupcakes, this is one of my favorites. I had it for the first time when I was visiting my cousin Iris in Monkton, Maryland, after a dinner of steamed Chesapeake Bay crabs and homemade coleslaw.

**MAKES: ABOUT 14–16 CUPCAKES**

PIE DOUGH
See Chocolate Cupcake Pie
  (page 152).

CHERRY ALMOND FILLING
$\frac{1}{2}$ cup/1 stick unsalted butter, room
  temperature
$\frac{1}{2}$ cup sugar
2 large eggs
1 cup ground almonds
Finely grated rind of 1 lemon
$2\frac{1}{2}$ cups pitted morello cherries
  (canned cherries work wonderfully
  well but you can use fresh or
  frozen, depending on the season)
Powdered sugar for dusting
Slivered almonds for decoration

1. Preheat oven to 350°F.

2. See Chocolate Cupcake Pie (page 152) for instructions on rolling out pie dough and lining molds.

3. Beat butter and sugar together until light and fluffy. Add eggs, one by one, beating well after each addition. Add ground almonds and lemon rind and mix well. Spoon mixture into pie shells, filling them about $\frac{1}{2}$ full. Press the cherries into the mixture, pushing them under the almond paste with your fingers.

4. Bake for 25–30 minutes until the surface is golden brown, puffed up, and springy to the touch. Turn off oven and leave cupcakes with door open for about 10 minutes. Remove from oven and let cool. Dust with powdered sugar and decorate with slivered almonds before serving.

# BAKLAVA Cups

The inspiration for these cupcakes is a wonderful and elegant dessert, found throughout North Africa and in every country around the Mediterranean basin.

**MAKES: ABOUT 12 CUPCAKES**

1 cup nuts (either walnuts, pistachios, or almonds, or a combination)
¼ cup toasted sesame seeds
1 teaspoon cinnamon
½ teaspoon cardamom
½ cup honey
1 tablespoon lemon juice
1 teaspoon orange blossom or rose water
8 ounces phyllo dough
½ cup/1 stick unsalted butter, melted and slightly cooled

1. Preheat oven to 350°F.

2. Coarsely chop nuts in a food processor. Transfer to a medium bowl and add sesame seeds, cinnamon, and cardamom. Mix well.

3. In a small pan, heat honey with lemon juice and orange blossom or rose water until just liquid and luke warm to the touch (do not cook). Pour mixture over nuts and stir well.

4. Cut phyllo dough into 5-inch squares. Put a square into each regular-size silicon cupcake mold. Brush with melted butter. Repeat five more times for each cupcake, staggering the corners of the square so that the sides of the molds are entirely covered. Flatten dough with the pastry brush as you go along. Put a heaping tablespoon of the nut and honey mixture in the center of each cupcake. Using a scissors or a very sharp knife, trim off excess dough to edge of cupcake molds or leave as is.

5. Bake for about 15–20 minutes until mixture is brown on top and dough is cooked. Remove from oven and cool. Carefully unmold Baklava Cups. They will harden as they cool in the mold. Serve in pretty cupcake papers.

**CUPCAKE TIP**
*Enjoy them with a cup of espresso or a glass of sweet mint tea after a meal or at tea time.*

# WHITE CHOCOLATE PANNA COTTA Cupcakes
## With Passion Fruit Sauce

Panna Cotta is an Italian egg cream that literally means "cooked cream." Technically, this recipe is not a real panna cotta since it calls for gelatin instead of egg yolks to set the cream. But this is a "no fail" recipe, easy to make and delicious served with Passion Fruit Sauce or a simple fruit sauce of your choice. If you have any fancy silicon cupcake molds with a design on top (sunflowers, roses, etc.), they would work particularly well.

**MAKES: ABOUT 8–10 CUPCAKES**

PANNA COTTA
1¼ cups heavy cream
¾ cup whole milk
5 ounces white chocolate, broken
    into pieces
¼ cup sugar
2 teaspoons unflavored gelatin
1 tablespoon water
PASSION FRUIT SAUCE
½ cup passion fruit pulp
1 cup sweet white wine (Sauternes or
    Muscat, for example)
¼ cup sugar

1. In a medium pan, mix the cream, milk, chocolate, and sugar. Gently heat mixture, stirring constantly, until it is smooth (do not boil).

2. Heat gelatin and water in a double boiler (over simmering but not boiling water) or a microwave. Stir until gelatin has dissolved and add to chocolate mixture.

3. Divide mixture between 8–10 silicon cupcake molds. Place in the refrigerator for about 3 hours until cream has set.

4. While cream is setting, mix the passion fruit pulp, wine, and sugar in a small pan. Bring to a boil, lower heat, and simmer for about 10 minutes without stirring, until mixture is reduced by about a third. Remove from heat and cool.

5. Unmold the panna cotta on individual plates and serve with Passion Fruit Sauce.

# BABA AU RHUM
## Cupcakes

These individual rum cakes are delicious with tea and make an elegant dessert, served with whipped cream or custard sauce. Use any size mold, depending on the desired effect. Mini-molds can be used to make bite-size baba that may be a bit messy to eat, but your guests will go away licking their fingers—and complimenting the chef!

**MAKES: ABOUT 12 CUPCAKES**

³/₄ cup, plus 1 tablespoon all-purpose flour

2 teaspoons baking powder

¹/₂ teaspoon salt, plus pinch for the egg whites

3 eggs, separated

1¹/₄ cups sugar

6 tablespoons hot milk

¹/₄ cup/¹/₂ stick unsalted butter, room temperature

1 teaspoon vanilla extract

SYRUP

2 cups water

²/₃ cup sugar

6 tablespoons rum

1 teaspoon vanilla extract

1. Preheat oven to 350°F.

2. Mix flour, baking powder, and salt together and set aside.

3. Using a mixer, cream egg yolks with sugar until the mixture is creamy and light in color. While the mixer is running, add hot milk, flour mixture, and butter and mix well. Add vanilla.

4. In a separate bowl, beat egg whites with a pinch of salt until stiff but not dry. Gently fold whites into batter. Pour batter into cupcake molds immediately, filling just ¹/₂ full. Cook for about 20 minutes or until brown on top. Leave babas in molds.

5. To make the syrup: in a medium pan, bring water and sugar to a boil and cook for 2 minutes. Remove from heat and add rum and vanilla. Slowly pour over babas, until all of the liquid is absorbed. Keep babas in their molds until they are to be served so that they soak up a maximum of syrup. You can keep them in the refrigerator for a few days after they have cooled but serve them at room temperature with a dollop of whipped cream or on a bed of custard sauce.

# BLUEBERRY TART
## Cupcakes

Once again, this pie was a great favorite at my restaurant. I usually made it in the fall with the fresh blueberries from the mountains nearby that inundated the village market at that time of the year. But frozen blueberries work at any time of the year.

**MAKES: ABOUT 14–16 REGULAR CUPCAKES OR 7–8 JUMBO CUPCAKES**

PIE DOUGH
See Chocolate Cupcake Pie (page 152).

BLUEBERRY FILLING
2 cups blueberries (if you are using frozen blueberries, don't defrost them)
1 cup heavy whipping cream
$^1/_2$ cup sugar
3 eggs
1 teaspoon vanilla extract
Whipped cream (optional)

1. Preheat oven to 350°F.

2. See Chocolate Cupcake Pie (page 152) for instructions on rolling out pie dough and lining molds. For jumbo molds cut out circles measuring 5 inches in diameter.

3. Divide blueberries up among pie shells, filling shells no more than $^1/_2$ full.

4. Beat cream, sugar, eggs, and vanilla together. Pour mixture over blueberries, filling shells about $^2/_3$ full. Bake for about 25 minutes or until cream has set. Cool cupcakes completely before removing from molds.

5. Serve with a dollop of whipped cream. If you are making the cupcakes in the silicon molds, serve them in pretty cupcake papers.

**CUPCAKE TIP**
*You can either use silicon molds or cupcake papers. Either work well.*

# STRUDEL Cups

Strudel is said to be a Viennese specialty but can be found throughout Eastern Europe.
I personally believe that it is the first cousin of baklava, probably brought to Europe by the
Turks during the reign of the Ottoman Empire. It is generally made with apples but works
well with cherries, ricotta cheese, apricots, or poppyseeds, just to name a few possible
ingredients. Here are a few different recipes that you can try.

**MAKES: ABOUT 12 CUPCAKES**

STRUDEL DOUGH
½ pound phyllo dough
½ cup/1 stick melted butter and
   slightly cooled

APPLE FILLING
2 cups peeled, cored, and chopped
   apple (about 4 medium apples)
2 tablespoons lemon juice
½ cup sugar (more or less to taste)
½ cup walnuts, chopped
¼ cup raisins
1 teaspoon cinnamon
¼ cup browned bread crumbs or
   ground almonds
Whipped cream (optional)

1. Preheat oven to 350°F.

2. Line regular silicon molds with the phyllo pastry according to the
directions for Baklava Cups (page 155).

3. To make the filling: place apple pieces in a large bowl. Add lemon juice
and coat apples well so that they don't turn brown. Add remaining filling
ingredients and mix well. The purpose of the bread crumbs or ground
almonds is to absorb the liquid. Proceed as with Baklava Cups using this
filling.

4. Serve individually on a plate with a dollop of whipped cream.

VARIATION: CHERRY FILLING

2 cups pitted sour cherries, fresh or frozen and defrosted (you can use
any type of cherry but the sour ones work the best), ½ cup sugar (more
or less to taste), ⅔ cup ground almonds, 1 teaspoon cinnamon.

VARIATION: RICOTTA FILLING

1½ cups ricotta cheese (you can substitute with cottage cheese), ¼ cup
sugar, 1 egg, slightly beaten, 3–5 tablespoons raisins, 2 teaspoons finely
grated lemon or orange rind.

# BOSTON CREAM
## Cupcakes

This cupcake is a variation of a Boston Cream Cake. The principle is two layers of a basic white cake, filled with custard, open on the sides (and a bit oozy!), and frosted on top.

**MAKES: ABOUT 18 REGULAR CUPCAKES OR 9 JUMBO CUPCAKES**

2 cups all-purpose cake flour
2 teaspoons baking powder
1 teaspoon salt
½ cup/1 stick unsalted butter, room
  temperature
1 cup sugar
3 egg yolks, well beaten
¾ cup milk
1 teaspoon vanilla extract
VANILLA CUSTARD FILLING
(CRÈME PATISSIÈRE)
1½ cups milk
1 vanilla bean (or 1 teaspoon vanilla
  extract)
½ cup sugar
¼ cup all-purpose flour
2 eggs, plus 2 yolks
Chocolate Ganache (page 81)

1. Preheat oven to 350°F.

2. Mix flour, baking powder, and salt together and set aside.

3. Cream butter and sugar until light and fluffy. Add egg yolks all at once and blend well. Alternately beat in dry ingredients and milk. Add vanilla.

4. Spoon batter directly into silicon cupcake molds, filling about ⅔ full. Bake for 20–25 minutes or until a tester inserted in the center comes out clean. Remove from oven and cool.

5. To make the filling: in a small pan, heat milk with vanilla. When milk boils, remove from heat. Just before you are ready to use the milk, remove the vanilla bean, split it in half lengthwise and scrape out the inside into the milk. Discard the bean.

6. In the top of a double boiler, combine sugar, flour, eggs, and yolks and whisk until light and creamy. Slowly add milk, stirring continually, and cook until mixture just starts to boil. Remove from heat and continue stirring for a few minutes to release steam and prevent mixture from continuing to cook. Cool completely before using.

7. Cut cupcakes in half. If you are using jumbo cupcakes, you can even cut them in thirds. Fill with Vanilla Custard Filling and frost the tops of the cupcakes with Chocolate Ganache.

# CARAMEL VERMICELLI
## Cupcake Flans

No, it isn't your imagination! You heard right. Cupcake flans made with vermicelli, the same pasta you put in your soup. Imagine the look on your guests' faces when you tell them what the main ingredient is!

**MAKES: ABOUT 16 CUPCAKES**

½ cup raisins
2 tablespoons rum
4 cups whole milk
1 cup sugar
1 cup vermicelli
4 eggs, separated
Pinch of salt
Caramel (either ready-made or homemade)
Crème Anglaise (page 164)
FOR DECORATION
Candied cherries
Walnuts, coarsely ground

**1.** Soak raisins in rum for 1 hour. Preheat oven to 350°F.

**2.** In a large pan, heat the milk with the sugar. When it starts to boil, add vermicelli and cook for 8–10 minutes, stirring continually. Remove pan from heat and let cool.

**3.** Add raisins, followed by egg yolks, one at a time, beating well after each addition.

**4.** Beat egg whites with salt until stiff but not dry. Gently fold into vermicelli mixture.

**5.** Put a little caramel into the bottom of each regular-size silicon cupcake mold (about ½ inch). Pour batter over caramel, filling cups ¾ full, and bake for about 15 minutes or until batter has set. Cool completely before unmolding.

**6.** Cover cupcakes with Crème Anglaise, decorate with candied cherries and ground walnuts, and serve individually.

**CUPCAKE TIP**
*If you are making your own caramel, use sugared cubes instead of loose sugar.*

# CLAFOUTIS WITH
## Crème Anglaise

A clafoutis is a very rustic French dessert, somewhere between a flan and a cake.
It can be made with any fruit but a "real" clafoutis is always made with cherries.

**MAKES: ABOUT 16 REGULAR CUPCAKES OR 8 JUMBO CUPCAKES**

¾ cup ground almonds
1¼ cups all-purpose flour
1½ teaspoons baking powder
1 teaspoon salt
½ cup/1 stick unsalted butter, room temperature
1 cup sugar
2 eggs, slightly beaten
½ cup milk
1 small shot glass cherry brandy (optional)
2 cups pitted cherries (if you are using frozen cherries don't defrost them)
Maraschino cherries for decoration
CRÈME ANGLAISE
  (VANILLA CUSTARD)
4 cups whole milk
1 vanilla bean or 1 teaspoon vanilla extract
6 egg yolks
½ cup sugar

1. Preheat oven to 350°F.

2. Mix almonds, flour, baking powder, and salt together and set aside.

3. Cream butter and sugar until light in color and fluffy. Add eggs, one at a time, mixing well after each addition. Alternately beat in dry ingredients and milk. Add cherry brandy. Beat batter until smooth. Fold in cherries.

4. Spoon batter into silicon cupcake molds, filling cups about ⅔ full. Bake for 20–25 minutes or until a tester inserted into the center comes out clean. Remove from oven, top with a maraschino cherry, and cool.

5. To make Crème Angaise: bring milk and vanilla to a boil in a medium pan and remove from heat. Just before you are ready to use the milk, remove the vanilla bean, split it in half lengthwise, and scrape out the inside into the milk. Discard the bean.

6. In a large bowl, combine egg yolks and sugar and mix well. Gradually add hot milk, stirring constinually. When all of the milk is used up and the mixture is smooth, return to pan and cook over very low heat, stirring continually. I always use a wooden spoon. The cream will thicken, little by little (do not boil). When the cream coats the back of the spoon, remove from heat and pour into another container. Stir for a few minutes to release the steam. Cool completely before serving.

# CHARLOTTE À LA FRAISE Cupcakes

These are the French equivalent of Strawberry Shortcake and delicious, especially when strawberries are in season. Many variations exist but the following is one of my favorites since the gelatin holds the cream together and it won't fall apart when unmolded.

**MAKES: ABOUT 12 JUMBO CHARLOTTES À LA FRAISE**

Flavoring (vanilla, kirsch, strawberry liqueur, etc.)
Sugar syrup (made by boiling 1 cup sugar with 1 cup water)
3 cups strawberries, hulled and chopped into little pieces or coarsely crushed
1 cup sugar
2 teaspoons gelatin (or equivalent)
3 tablespoons cold water
3 tablespoons boiling water
1 tablespoon lemon juice
1½ cups whipped cream
1 package ladyfingers (I prefer the spongy ones to the dry ones because they soak up the liquid better)
Strawberry sauce (page 168) to serve

1. Add flavoring to sugar syrup. Set aside and cool.

2. In a large bowl, mix chopped or crushed strawberries and sugar.

3. In a small bowl, soak gelatin in 3 tablespoons cold water until it is soft. Add 3 tablespoons boiling water and stir until the gelatin is dissolved. Add to strawberries and mix well. Add lemon juice. When mixture starts to set, gently fold in whipped cream.

4. To assemble, quickly dip ladyfingers in cooled sugar syrup (you don't want them to be soggy) and line jumbo silicon cupcake molds, bottom and sides, cutting to fit tightly. Fill lined molds with strawberry cream and put in the refrigerator overnight.

5. Carefully run a dull knife around the edges and unmold on individual plates. Serve with Strawberry Sauce (page 168).

**CUPCAKE TIP**
*You can replace the lemon juice with orange juice. Or the sugar syrup with orange juice, as for Chocolate Charlotte (page 182). This will cut the sweetness a little and the orange flavor will go well with the strawberries.*

# BLACK FOREST Cupcakes

The inspiration for these cupcakes, a traditional German cake, *Schwarzwälderkirschtorte*, are a mouthwatering combination of chocolate, cherries, and whipped cream.

**MAKES: ABOUT 16–18 REGULAR CUPCAKES OR 8 JUMBO CUPCAKES**

1²/₃ cups all-purpose flour
2 teaspoons baking powder
1 teaspoon salt
²/₃ cup unsweetened cocoa powder
¹/₂ cup/1 stick unsalted butter, room temperature
1¹/₂ cups sugar
2 eggs
1¹/₂ cups milk
1 teaspoon vanilla extract
¹/₂ cup kirsch or cherry brandy (optional but highly recommended!)

FILLING AND FROSTING
1 cup heavy whipping cream
1 cup powdered sugar
¹/₂ teaspoon vanilla extract
1 tablespoon kirsch or cherry brandy (optional)
1 can pitted cherries, drained
Grated dark chocolate for sprinkling

1. Preheat oven to 350°F.

2. Mix flour, baking powder, salt, and cocoa together and set aside.

3. Cream butter and sugar until light and fluffy. Add eggs, one at a time, mixing well after each addition. Alternately add flour mixture and milk. Add vanilla and beat well.

4. Spoon batter into cupcake papers, filling cups about ²/₃ full. Bake for 25 minutes or until a tester inserted into the center comes out clean. Remove from oven and cool.

5. When cupcakes are cool, unmold, cut in half or in thirds, and sprinkle with cherry liqueur.

6. To make the filling and frosting: in a large bowl, whip the cream until it forms soft peaks. Add sugar, vanilla, and kirsch. Beat until stiff. Spread layer(s) of cake with half the filling. Press cherries into whipped cream before adding next layer. Save enough cherries to decorate cupcakes. Frost top and sides of cupcakes with whipped cream. Decorate with remaining cherries. Sprinkle grated chocolate over cupcakes and serve individually in a pretty cupcake paper.

**CUPCAKE TIP**
*You can replace the canned cherries with Maraschino cherries if preferred.*

# CUPCAKE KEBABS

This variation on the cupcake theme is perfect for a party or for an elegant dessert, depending on the desired effect. Just about any cupcake recipe that you can use for making mini-cupcakes will do. Following are two different variations on the theme.

**MAKES: ABOUT 12 KEBABS**

MINI-CUPCAKES
White Fondant Glaze (page 142) or
  ready-made fondant
Food coloring (3 different ones)
Gummy candies or fresh fruit
Bamboo skewers

STRAWBERRY SAUCE
2 cups strawberries
½ cup sugar
¼ cup water
A few drops lemon juice
Whipped cream for decoration

**CUPCAKE TIP**
*This strawberry sauce
can be kept in the
refrigerator or frozen
for later use.*

1. Follow the recipe for Lamingtons (page 178), Mini-financiers (page 110) or Genoise (page 175).

2. Either make your own fondant (see recipe for Christmas Cupcake, page 142) or use ready-made fondant, following manufacturer's instructions. Divide fondant into three bowls and put a different food coloring in each. Dip cupcakes in fondant and drain on a rack.

3. Assemble cupcakes, three to a skewer (one of each color), alternating with the following decorations:

VARIATION: PARTY CUPCAKE KEBABS

Alternate the cupcakes with gummy candies. Arrange the skewers attractively on a plate, surrounded by gummy candies. These Cupcakes-on-a-Stick will be a great addition to any child's party.

VARIATION: DESSERT CUPCAKE KEBABS

Alternating the cupcakes with fresh fruit. Wash and clean the strawberries. Slowly heat the strawberries and sugar in a medium pan with water. When mixture starts to boil, cook for 1 minute and remove from heat. Purée by hand or in a food processor with a few drops of lemon juice. Cool before serving. Ladle a little Strawberry Sauce in a plate and lay a skewer over the sauce. Put remaining Strawberry Sauce in a bowl so that your guests can serve themselves. The idea is similar to a fondue.

# ROSEMARY'S SUMMER PUDDING Cupcakes

This recipe was passed on to me by Rosemary, an Irish woman living in the south of France, who made it for me for lunch one beautiful sunny day in her village, perched between the Mediterranean and the Cevennes mountains.

**MAKES: ABOUT 8 JUMBO CUPCAKES**

4 cups summer fruits (black and red currants, cherries, strawberries, raspberries, blackberries, rhubarb, etc.)
½ cup sugar (to taste, depending on the sweetness of the fruit used)
5–6 tablespoons water
About 8–10 thin slices of white bread, crusts removed
Whipped or liquid cream
Mint sprigs for decoration (optional)

1. In a large pan, gently cook fruit, sugar, and water until sugar is just melted. Fruits should hold their shape so don't overcook. Remove from heat and cool slightly.

2. Cut rounds of white bread to fit the bottom of jumbo silicon cupcake molds. Cut bread to line the sides. You want the entire inside of the mold to be covered, fitting the bread neatly together. Carefully scoop fruit into lined cupcakes, saving a little of the juice. Cut the remaining bread to form a lid and cover the fruit, pressing the bread into the fruit so that it absorbs the liquid. Cover with aluminum foil and place in the refrigerator overnight.

3. When ready to serve, invert onto a serving dish and pour a little of the reserved liquid over each cupcake. The fruit will have completely saturated the bread and it will be a wonderful dark purple color. Serve with whipped or liquid cream and a sprig of mint.

**CUPCAKE TIP**
*I have found that frozen berry mixtures work particularly well*

# CHOC & NUT Dacquoise

A "Dacquoise" is a classic French pastry of baked nut meringues layered with butter cream. Here, the meringue is made with almonds and hazelnuts with a chocolate ganache filling.

**1.** Make the meringues following Almond and Hazelnut Mini-Meringues (page 150), using regular silicon molds instead of mini-cupcake molds. Put about ¹/₂ inch of the uncooked meringue in the bottom of a mold. (You can also trace circles the diameter of a cupcake on a piece of wax paper. Turn the paper over, place it on a rigid ovenproof dish and pipe or spread meringue over the circle, about ¹/₂ inch thick.)

**2.** Bake until meringue is golden brown and firm to the touch. Wait until it has entirely cooled to unmold.

**3.** To make the ganache: place chocolate and cream in a double boiler and heat until cream is warm to the touch and the chocolate starts to melt. Remove from heat and stir until all of the chocolate has melted and the mixture is homogeneous. Remember—you don't want to cook the chocolate, you just want to melt it. Place bowl in cold water. When chocolate is cool to the touch, beat ganache for about 10 minutes with an electric beater until the color lightens and soft shiny peaks form.

**4.** To assemble: when the disks are cool, line a cupcake mold with pretty cupcake papers. Place a disk in the bottom of each cupcake paper. Spread or pipe a layer of ganache over the disk and place a second disk on top, lightly pressing it into the ganache. Cover the cupcake tin with plastic and put it in the refrigerator for at least 2 hours until the ganache has set. Dust with powdered sugar before serving.

**MAKES: ABOUT 10 CUPCAKES**

Almond and Hazelnut Meringues
  (page 150)
WHIPPED CHOCOLATE GANACHE
6 ounces dark chocolate, broken into
  little pieces
³/₄ cup heavy cream
Powdered sugar for dusting

**CUPCAKE TIP**
*You can also
assemble these cupcakes
in silicon molds without
cupcake papers or in no
mold at all.*

# GELÉE OF FRUIT WITH WHITE WINE IN A Cupcake

This surprising dessert lends itself well to a cupcake format. Basically, it is a fruit salad in white wine jelly, an ideal and elegant dessert for any season, depending on the fruit that is available. It will be a perfect and light ending to a gourmet meal.

**MAKES: ABOUT 12 REGULAR CUPCAKES OR 6 JUMBO CUPCAKES**

3 cups of fresh fruit, washed and cut into small pieces (pears, cherries, strawberries, bananas, pineapple, peaches, apricots, oranges, apples, etc.)
1 heaping tablespoon unflavored gelatin (or equivalent)
1 cup water
½ cup sugar
1 cup dry white wine
1 tablespoon lemon juice
Whipped cream

1. Prepare fruits. Place fruits on a paper towel or a clean dish towel to absorb extra moisture.

2. Dissolve gelatin in ½ cup water in a double boiler. After it has dissolved, remove it from the heat but keep it over hot water.

3. In a large bowl, mix remaining water, sugar, wine, and lemon juice. Stir with a whisk until all of the sugar has dissolved. Add gelatin and continue stirring. Pour ¼ inch of the liquid into each cup of a silicon cupcake mold (either regular or jumbo). Put mold in refrigerator until gelatin has set (about 1 hour).

4. Remove from refrigerator and fill cups with mixed fruits. Pour remaining gelatin mixture over fruits, covering them with ¼ inch of the liquid. Put mold back in the refrigerator for at least 6 hours.

5. To unmold, run a dull knife (very carefully!) around the edges of the mold and unmold onto a serving platter. Keep in the refrigerator until you are ready to serve. Serve on individual plates with whipped cream.

# DESSERT
# Cups

Dessert Cups are hard chocolate cups made in a cupcake paper. They can be made with dark chocolate, milk chocolate, or white chocolate. The white chocolate cups are wonderful filled with fresh berries and the dark cups are delicious with raspberries. Fill any of them with candy for a party and set them in pretty cupcake papers.

**MAKES: ABOUT 12 CUPS**

15 ounces white chocolate
2 cups fresh or defrosted frozen
  berries (raspberries, strawberries, etc.)
Sugar to taste
Raspberry sauce (see page 96)
Whipped cream (optional)

1. Melt the chocolate over a double boiler or in a microwave.

2. Using a pastry brush, coat inside of a cupcake paper set in a muffin tin with melted chocolate (chocolate should be cool to the touch but of good spreading consistency). Put muffin tin in the refrigerator for about 20 minutes or until chocolate has hardened. Take it out of the refrigerator and add another coat. You may need to set chocolate over warm water or put it back in the microwave again to get it to the right consistency. Put cups back in refrigerator again so that the chocolate can harden. If you want sturdier cups, add a third coat.

3. When the cups are hard, peel off paper very carefully. You can keep these cups in a cool dry place or freeze them for future use.

4. Fill cups with berries, sprinkle with sugar, and drizzle with raspberry sauce. Add a dollop of whipped cream, if desired.

# SPECIAL OCCASION
## Cupcakes

These cupcakes are perfect for special occasions such as birthdays, weddings, graduations, or showers. The principle is that they are made of two cupcakes made in a silicon mold—a regular size and a mini-size—assembled, frosted with fondant and decorated for the occasion, whatever it may be.

**MAKES: 10 REGULAR AND 10 MINI-CUPCAKES**

GENOISE CUPCAKE
1¼ cups sugar
6 eggs
1⅔ cups all-purpose flour
½ cup/1 stick unsalted butter, melted and slightly cooled (but still warm to the touch)
Flavoring (vanilla, almond extract, etc.)
FOOD COLORING (OPTIONAL)
White Fondant Glaze (page 142)

1. Preheat oven to 350°F.

2. Put sugar and eggs in a double boiler over simmering water. Using a whisk or a hand-held beater (electric or otherwise), beat mixture constantly as it heats until it is lemony in color and forms soft peaks. The whole procedure should take about 10–15 minutes. Remove from heat and very gently fold in the flour, butter, and flavoring with a whisk.

3. Carefully spoon batter into regular and mini-silicon molds (you will need the same number of each), filling about ⅔ full. Bake for about 20 minutes, a shorter time for the mini-cupcakes, or until a tester inserted into the center comes out clean and cupcakes are just slightly golden on top. Remove from oven and cool.

4. Add food coloring to the fondant, depending on occasion. (For instance, you can use red and/or blue food coloring for a baby shower.) Set some of the fondant aside for dipping the mini-cupcakes.

5. To assemble: frost cooled regular-size cupcakes with fondant. Dip mini cupcake in the fondant and place on top of regular cupcake. Decorate.

# FAR BRETON
## Cupcakes

A Far Breton is a specialty from Brittany, in the Celtic northwest corner of France. It is a rather rustic flan, made with prunes, a perfect dessert for winter when fresh fruits are rare. I suggest making these cupcakes in a silicon cupcake mold so that they can be easily unmolded and served luke warm with Vanilla Custard flavored with a little rum.

**MAKES: ABOUT 12 CUPCAKES**

12 pitted prunes
1 small glass of rum for soaking
    prunes (about ¼ cup)
¾ cup all-purpose flour
Pinch of salt
½ cup sugar
2 eggs, slightly beaten
1½ cups whole milk
2 tablespoons/¼ stick unsalted
    butter, melted and cooled
Powdered sugar for dusting
Vanilla custard (page 164) to serve

1. In a bowl, soak prunes in rum for about an hour, turning from time to time. Drain liquid and save. Set prunes aside.

2. Preheat oven to 350°F.

3. In a large bowl, mix the flour, salt, and sugar. Beat eggs with milk and butter and add liquid to dry ingredients, mixing well with a wooden spoon or an electric mixer. Batter will be liquid. Stir in 2 tablespoons of the liquid from the prunes.

4. Place a prune in each cup of a regular silicon cupcake mold and fill just ½ full. Cook for about 35 minutes or until brown on top. Batter will rise and then deflate when it cools. Remove from oven and cool.

5. Sprinkle with powdered sugar and serve on a plate with Vanilla Custard (page 164) to which you have added a little of the rum used for soaking the prunes.

**CUPCAKE TIP**
*Alternatively,
just serve them in a
pretty cupcake paper
dusted with
powdered sugar.*

# LAMINGTON
## Mini-Cupcakes

A Lamington is a small square of plain white cake or sponge cake, dipped in melted chocolate and sugar and coated with shredded coconut. It is a specialty of Australia.

**MAKES: ABOUT 40 MINI-CUPCAKES**

2 cups all-purpose flour
2 teaspoons baking powder
1 teaspoon salt
¼ cup/½ stick unsalted butter, room temperature
¾ cup sugar
2 eggs
1 teaspoon vanilla extract
½ cup milk
2 cups shredded coconut, toasted for extra flavor

CHOCOLATE ICING
3 tablespoons boiling water
1 tablespoon unsalted butter
¼ cup unsweetened cocoa powder
2 cups powdered sugar

1. Preheat oven to 350°F. Mix flour, baking powder, and salt and set aside.

2. Cream butter and sugar together until light and fluffy. Add eggs, one at a time, mixing well after each addition. Blend in vanilla. Alternately add flour mixture and milk and beat until batter is smooth.

3. Spoon batter into silicon mini-cupcake molds, a heaping teaspoon of batter per mini-cupcake. Cook for about 15 minutes or until brown on top. Remove from oven and cool.

4. Spread out coconut on a piece of wax paper or in a large shallow bowl and set aside.

5. To make the icing: pour boiling water over butter. Add cocoa and mix well. Gradually add sugar and beat until mixture is smooth with a whisk or a wooden spoon. The chocolate should be smooth and glossy (it should also be thin enough to easily cover the cupcakes—add extra boiling water if necessary).

6. Using two forks or prongs, dip the cupcakes into the chocolate and roll in the coconut. Set cupcakes on a cake rack until they have cooled. These cupcakes freeze well.

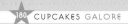
# PARTY SUNDAE
## Cupcakes

Serve these cupcakes as you would a sundae, in an ice cream dish, with all the trimmings. I have given a recipe for Hot Fudge Sauce but you can use any sauce you wish.

**MAKES: 16 CUPCAKES**

VANILLA PEANUT CUPCAKE
2 cups all-purpose flour
2 teaspoons baking powder
½ cup/1 stick unsalted butter, room temperature
⅔ cup light brown sugar
2 eggs
1 teaspoon vanilla extract
¾ cup milk
½ cup coarsely chopped salted peanuts

HOT FUDGE SAUCE
1 cup whipping cream
¼ cup light corn syrup
12 ounces good quality chocolate (at least 55% cocoa solids)
2 tablespoons/¼ stick unsalted butter, room temperature
1 teaspoon vanilla extract
Ice cream of your choice
Chopped peanuts, Whipped cream, Maraschino cherries for decoration

1. Preheat oven to 350°F.

2. Mix flour and baking powder together and set aside.

3. Cream butter and sugar until light and fluffy. Add eggs, one at a time, mixing well after each addition. Alternately beat in flour mixture, milk, and vanilla extract. Fold in peanuts.

4. Spoon batter into regular silicon cupcake molds, filling about ⅔ full. Bake for 20–25 minutes or until a tester inserted in the center comes out clean. Remove from oven and cool.

5. To make the sauce: in a pan, slowly heat cream, corn syrup, and chocolate, stirring constantly. Simmer for 5–10 minutes or until mixture starts to thicken. Remove from heat and stir in butter and vanilla. Cool slightly before using. You can keep this sauce in the refrigerator and gently reheat it before using.

6. Using a sharp knife, cut a wide shallow hole in the top of each cupcake, the width of a scoop of ice cream, and just deep enough to hold it. Put cupcake in an ice cream dish, fill with a scoop of ice cream and pour the fudge sauce over the cupcake. Top with chopped peanuts, whipped cream, and a maraschino cherry.

# OPERA Cupcakes

An "Opera" is a traditional French pastry found in the finest pastry shops across France. It is not difficult to make but requires a bit of time and patience. The traditional cake usually comes in the form of a layered sheet cake cut into rectangles. A true "Opera" will have a little piece of gold leaf (edible, of course) on top. This is a somewhat simplified version.

MAKES: **ABOUT 12 REGULAR CUPCAKES OR 6 JUMBO CUPCAKES**

GIOCONDA BISCUIT (BISCUIT JOCONDE)—THE TRADITIONAL CAKE RECIPE USED TO MAKE THE PASTRY):
2 tablespoons/¼ stick unsalted butter
½ cup finely ground almonds
⅔ cup, plus 2 tablespoons sugar
¼ cup all-purpose flour
4 eggs, separated
Pinch of salt
Chocolate Ganache (page 171) made using 4 ounces chocolate and ½ cup heavy cream
½ quantity Mocha Butter Cream Frosting (page 70)
Edible gold leaf or glitter sugar for decoration

1. Preheat oven to 250°F.

2. Melt butter and set aside until cool.

3. Beat almonds, ⅔ cup sugar, flour, and egg yolks until the mixture is light and foamy (at least 10 minutes).

4. In a separate bowl, beat egg whites with salt and remaining sugar until they are stiff but not dry. Gently fold into almond mixture. Delicately add cooled melted butter, using a spatula or a whisk.

5. Fill silicon cupcake molds just a little over half way. Bake for about 10 minutes or until brown on top. Be careful not to burn these cupcakes—they will cook quickly.

6. Unmold when cupcakes are cool and cut into three equal layers.

7. Beat half of the ganache with an electric beater for about 5–10 minutes until it is light and fluffy. If the other half hardens before you can use it, set it over warm water until it is of the right consistency.

8. To assemble, spread Mocha Buttercream Icing on the first layer. Add second layer and spread beaten Chocolate Ganache. Add third layer and frost with liquid ganache. Decorate with a piece of edible gold leaf or glitter sugar and serve in pretty cupcake papers.

# CHOCOLATE CHARLOTTE Cupcakes

When I had my restaurant in the south of France, Chocolate Charlotte was by far the most popular dessert we made and I had to make one every day or my customers would go away disappointed. This is the cupcake version of that very charlotte.

**MAKES: ABOUT 8–10 JUMBO CUPCAKES**

8 ounces dark chocolate
½ cup/1 stick unsalted butter, cut into small pieces
½ cup sugar
3 eggs, separated
½ cup whipping cream
Pinch of salt
1 package ladyfingers (I prefer the spongy ones to the dry ones because they soak up the liquid better)
Orange juice
FOR DECORATION
Custard or Raspberry Sauce (page 96)
Roses and extra chocolate sauce

1. Melt chocolate, butter, and sugar in a double boiler, until chocolate is just melted. Remove from heat immediately and add egg yolks, one at a time, beating well after each addition. Set mixture aside and let cool. When mixture is cool, pour in cream. The mixture will seize up a bit and thicken.

2. Beat egg whites with a pinch of salt until stiff but not dry. Gently fold into chocolate mixture.

3. To assemble, briefly dip ladyfingers in orange juice—you don't want them to be soggy. Line the sides of the jumbo silicon cupcake molds, cutting ladyfingers to size and squeezing them together tightly. Fill lined molds with chocolate mixture to just a little below the top. Cover cupcakes with more ladyfingers dipped in orange juice, fitting them well to cover all of the chocolate. Place mold in refrigerator overnight.

4. Unmold onto a serving dish and serve upside down, either in a pretty cupcake paper or on a plate with custard and/or Raspberry Sauce (page 96).

# AUNT FLORENCE'S FROZEN LEMON Cupcakes

This recipe comes to me from my cousin Deborah (via her cousin Jocelyn) whose mother (my Aunt Florence) used to make them for her for as a special treat. Deborah tells me that she used to make them as well until she realized how bad whipping cream was for the health. So throw caution to the wind and make these very easy and elegant cupcakes for that special occasion.

**MAKES: ABOUT 12 CUPCAKES**

LEMON CREAM
1 cup sugar
Juice and finely grated rind of 1
    lemon
2 cups whipping cream
CRUST
1/4 cup/1/2 stick unsalted butter, room
    temperature
1/2 cup crushed graham crackers
1/2 cup crushed corn flakes
2 tablespoons sugar
Jellied lemon slices for decoration

1. To make the lemon cream: combine sugar and lemon juice and rind in a large bowl. Gradually beat in cream.

2. To make the crust: melt butter in a pan over low heat and stir in crushed graham crackers, corn flakes, and sugar.

3. Place crust mixture in the bottom of cupcake molds. Pour lemon cream on top. Freeze for at least 3 hours. Unmold, top with a jellied lemon slice, and serve.

**CUPCAKE TIP**
*You can use
cupcake papers or make
these frozen cupcakes in
either a rigid or a
silicon mold.*

# INDEX

## A

after eight cupcakes 81

almonds

  almond & hazelnut mini
  meringues 150

  almond butter cream
    frosting 121

  the Arlésienne 94

  Bourdaloue cupcakes 87

  cherry almond pie cupcakes 154

  choc & nut Dacquoise 171

  clafoutis with crème Anglais 164

  Epiphany cupcakes 121

  linzertorte cupcakes 102

  mendiant cupcakes 103

  mini-financier cupcakes 110

  opera cupcakes 181

  Orient Express cupcakes 108

  saffron & orange cupcakes 115

  zucchini pine nut cupcakes 18

American parfait icing 130

anise butter cream frosting 78

apples

  apple-cranberry crumble
    cupcakes 28

  caramelized apples 84

  deep-dish apple pie
    cupcakes 151

  strudel cups 161

  tarte tatin cupcakes 84

  Thanksgiving apple cider
    cupcakes 134

apricots 94

Arlésienne, the 94

Aunt Florence's frozen lemon
  cupcakes 185

## B

baba au rhum cupcakes 158

baking tips 11

Baklava cups 155

banana split cupcakes 56

beer & peanuts cupcakes 65

birthday beauties 46

black & white cupcakes 20

black currants

  Kir cupcakes 66

  Rosemary's summer pudding
  cupcakes 170

Black Forest cupcakes 167

blackberries 170

blueberries

  blue blueberry 'n' cream
    cupcakes 22

  blueberry tart cupcakes 159

July 4th blueberry & raspberry cupcakes 132

Boston cream cupcakes 162

bourbon 71

Bourdaloue cupcakes 87

brandy

Christmas fruit cupcakes 142

midnight madness cupcakes 76

brownie cupcakes 24

Burgundy blues cupcakes 62

butter rum frosting 64

## C

cappuccino cupcakes 68

caramel vermicelli cupcake flans 163

caramelized apples 84

carrots 133

Cevenol cupcakes 88

champagne 144

Chanukah honey hazelnut cupcakes 140

Charlotte à la fraise cupcakes 166

cherries

Black Forest cupcakes 167

cherry almond pie cupcakes 154

clafoutis with crème Anglais 164

pineapple surprises 106

Rosemary's summer pudding cupcakes 170

Valentine' Day cupcakes 120

chestnuts 88

chocolate

after eight cupcakes 81

basic chocolate cupcakes 52

birthday beauties 46

black & white cupcakes 20

Black Forest cupcakes 167

brownie cupcakes 24

Burgundy blues cupcakes 62

choc & nut Dacquoise 171

chocolate & peanut butter cupcakes 25

Chocolate Charlotte cupcakes 182

chocolate coconut cupcakes 19

chocolate cupcake pies 152

chocolate fudge frosting 56

chocolate ganache 81

chocolate hazelnut cupcakes 44

chocolate malted milk shake cupcakes 58

chocolate mousse cupcakes 90

chocolate sundae cupcakes 48

Christmas peppermint chocolate cupcakes 141

cookies 'n' cream cupcakes 49

Day of the Dead choc cinnamon cupcakes 138

dessert cups 174

dessert rose cupcakes 148

Earl Grey cupcakes 92

hot chocolate & marshmallows cupcakes 50

July 4th red velvet cupcakes 130

lamington mini cupcakes 178

macadamia & white chocolate cupcakes 107

Marrakech moments 104

mezzo-mezzo cupcakes 72

midnight madness cupcakes 76

mint julep cupcakes 71

opera cupcakes 181

Poire Belle Helene 111

rocky road cupcakes 54

s'mores cupcakes 57

Valentines' Day cupcakes 120

white chocolate & raspberry
cupcakes 112
white chocolate panna cotta
cupcakes 156
Christmas fruit cupcakes 142
Christmas peppermint chocolate
cupcakes 141
cider 134
cinnamon and spice frosting 133
cinnamon butter frosting 138
clafoutis with crème Anglais 164
coconut
chocolate coconut cupcakes 19
lamington mini cupcakes 178
Pina Colada cupcakes 77
pineapple surprises 106
Yetti cupcakes 42

coffee
cappuccino cupcakes 68
Irish coffee cupcakes 70
mezzo-mezzo cupcakes 72
tiramisu cupcakes 101
cookies 'n' cream cupcakes 49
cranberries
apple-cranberry crumble
cupcakes 28
Thanksgiving carrot, cranberry &
nut cupcakes 133
cream cheese frosting 18
cream chocolate sauce 111
crème Anglaise 164
crème brulée cupcakes 93
Crepe Suzette cupcakes 89
Cuba Libre cupcakes 69
cupcake papers 13
cupcake tins 12
cupcake kebabs 168
currants 124

**D**

Day of the Dead choc cinnamon
cupcakes 138
decorations 14–15

deep-dish apple pie cupcakes 151
dessert cups 174
dessert rose cupcakes 148

**E**

Earl Grey cupcakes 92
Easter lavender butterfly
cupcakes 129
Easter lemon chiffon cupcakes 126
Epiphany cupcakes 121
equipment 12–13

**F**

Far Breton cupcakes 176
figs
the Languedocienne 98
mendiant cupcakes 103
frosting 14–15
fruit
dessert cups 174
fruit yogurt cupcakes 36
gelée of fruit with white wine in
a cupcake 172
Rosemary's summer pudding
cupcakes 170
*see also* apples etc

## G

gateau de Savoie 114

gelée of fruit with white wine in a
cupcake 172

Genoise cupcakes 175

ginger 30

glazes 14–15

goat cheese frosting 98

graham cracker and milk chocolate
cupcakes 57

grapefruit 38

green tea cupcakes 108

## H

Halloween orange juice
cupcakes 136

Halloween pumpkin pecan
cupcakes 137

hazelnuts

almond & hazelnut mini
meringues 150

Chanukah honey hazelnut
cupcakes 140

choc & nut Dacquoise 171

chocolate hazelnut cupcakes 44

linzertorte cupcakes 102

mendiant cupcakes 103

honey

Baklava cups 155

Chanukah honey hazelnut
cupcakes 140

the Languedocienne 98

poppyseed & lavender honey
cupcakes 37

hot chocolate & marshmallows
cupcakes 50

hot fudge sauce 180

## I

icing 14–15

ingredients 10–11

Irish coffee cupcakes 70

## J

jelly

the Arlésienne 94

Christmas fruit cupcakes 142

Easter lavender butterfly
cupcakes 129

jelly-filled cupcakes 52

Kir cupcakes 66

mini-financier cupcakes 110

Mother's Day filled rose
cupcakes 125

peanut butter & jelly swirls 53

strawberry & rhubarb crisp
cupcakes 34

strawberry-filled oatmeal
cupcakes 32

July 4th blueberry & raspberry
cupcakes 132

July 4th red velvet cupcakes 130

## K

Kir cupcakes 66

## L

lamington mini cupcakes 178

Languedocienne, the 98

lemons

Aunt Florence's frozen lemon
cupcakes 185

birthday beauties 46

Christmas fruit cupcakes 142

Easter lavender butterfly
cupcakes 129

Easter lemon chiffon
cupcakes 126

lemon meringue pie cupcakes 26

sunshine & vitamin C
  cupcakes 38

limes

  margarita cupcakes 75

  ricotta lime cupcakes 99

linzertorte cupcakes 102

## M

macadamia nuts 107

maple syrup 29

margarita cupcakes 75

Marrakech moments 104

marsala 101

marshmallows

  hot chocolate & marshmallow
    cupcakes 50

rocky road cupcakes 54

s'mores cupcakes 57

Yeti cupcakes 42

mascarpone cream 101

mendiant cupcakes 103

mezzo-mezzo cupcakes 72

midnight madness
  cupcakes 76

mini-financier cupcakes 110

mint

  after eight cupcakes 81

  mint julep cupcakes 71

mocha butter cream frosting 70

Mother's Day filled rose
  cupcakes 125

## N

New Year's Eve confetti
  cupcakes 145

New Year's Eve pink champagne
  cupcakes 144

no-cook marshmallow icing 57

nuts

  Baklava cups 155

  persimmon nut harvest treat 33

  *see also* almonds etc

## O

oatmeal

  St. Patrick's Day Irish soda bread
    cupcakes 124

  strawberry-filled oatmeal
    cupcakes 32

old-fashioned fudge frosting 48

opera cupcakes 181

oranges

  Christmas fruit cupcakes 142

  Crepe Suzette cupcakes 89

  Halloween orange juice
    cupcakes 136

  Marrakech moments 104

  orange cream cheese frosting 33

  saffron & orange cupcakes 115

  sunshine & vitamin C
    cupcakes 38

Orient Express cupcakes 108

## P

papers, for cupcakes 13

party sundae cupcakes 180

passion fruit 156

pastel cupcake frosting 46

pastis cupcakes 78

peaches 96

peanut butter

chocolate & peanut butter
cupcakes 25

peanut butter & jelly swirls 53

peanuts

beer & peanuts cupcakes 65

party sundae cupcakes 180

pears

Bourdaloue cupcakes 87

Poire Belle Helene 111

pecan nuts 137

péche melba cupcakes 96

peppermint 141

persimmon nut harvest treats 33

Pina Colada cupcakes 77

pine nuts 18

pineapple

Pina Colada cupcakes 77

pineapple surprises 106

pistachio nuts

mini-financier cupcakes 110

St. Patrick's Day pistachio yogurt
cupcakes 122

Poire Belle Helene 111

poppyseed & lavender honey
cupcakes 37

prunes 176

pumpkin 137

**R**

raisins

mendiant cupcakes 103

rum raisin cupcakes 64

St. Patrick's Day Irish soda bread
cupcakes 124

strudel cups 161

raspberries

the Arlésienne 94

July 4th blueberry & raspberry
cupcakes 132

péche melba cupcakes 96

Rosemary's summer pudding
cupcakes 170

white chocolate & raspberry
cupcakes 112

real vanilla cupcakes 48

red currants 170

rhubarb

Rosemary's summer pudding
cupcakes 170

strawberry & rhubarb crisp
cupcakes 34

ricotta lime cupcakes 99

rocky road cupcakes 54

root beer float 45

rose syrup 125

Rosemary's summer pudding
cupcakes 170

rum

baba au rhum cupcakes 158

Cuba Libre cupcakes 69

midnight madness cupcakes 76

Pina Colada cupcakes 77

rum raisin cupcakes 64

**S**

saffron & orange cupcakes 115

Savoy cake 114

s'mores cupcakes 57

snow frosting 42

special occasion cupcakes 175

St. Patrick's Day Irish soda bread cupcakes 124

St. Patrick's Day pistachio yogurt cupcakes 122

steamed coffee frosting 68

strawberries

  birthday beauties 46

  Charlotte à la fraise cupcakes 166

  cupcakes kebabs 168

  strawberry & rhubarb crisp cupcakes 34

  strawberry cheesecake 116

strudel cups 161

sunshine & vitamin C cupcakes 38

## T

tarte tatin cupcakes 84

tea

  Christmas peppermint chocolate cupcakes 141

  Earl Grey cupcakes 92

  Orient Express cupcakes 108

tequila 75

Thanksgiving apple cider cupcakes 134

Thanksgiving carrot, cranberry & nut cupcakes 133

three citrus fruit custard 38

three-gingerbread cupcake 30

tins, for cupcakes 12

tiramisu cupcakes 101

toppings 14–15

## V

Valentine's Day cupcakes 120

vanilla cupcakes, real 48

vermicelli 163

## W

walnuts

  brownie cupcakes 24

  maple walnut delight 29

  rocky road cupcakes 54

  strudel cups 161

  Thanksgiving carrot & cranberry cupcakes 133

whiskey

  Irish coffee cupcakes 70

  St. Patrick's Day Irish soda bread cupcakes 124

white chocolate

  white chocolate & raspberry cupcakes 112

  white chocolate cream cheese frosting 48

  white chocolate mint frosting 71

  white chocolate panna cotta cupcakes 156

white velvet cupcakes 42

## Y

yellow cupcakes, basic 52

Yeti cupcakes 42

'yin-yang' frosting 108

yogurt cupcakes 36

## Z

zucchini pine nut cupcakes 18